Meaningful wisdom to guide and in _____ _____ ___ lives of others. Not only will this bc ____ _____ _____ change the lives of the people who f ____ __ _____ __ you.

—CRAIG GROESCHEL, PASTOR, LIFE.CHURCH;
NEW YORK TIMES BESTSELLING AUTHOR

Speaks to the part of each of us that is agitated by injustice. Be prepared to be agitated in the best way. Get ready to move into a radical stage called transformation. Reminds us how simple it is once we make room for disruptive compassion.

—JOEL SMALLBONE, KING AND COUNTRY,
AND MORIAH SMALLBONE, TRALA

I've had many opportunities to interact with Convoy of Hope. Each time, I have come away moved, inspired, changed, and motivated to become more involved in their work. I hope this book inspires many people to reach out and serve others.

—DR. HENRY CLOUD, CLINICAL PSYCHOLOGIST,
LEADERSHIP EXPERT, AUTHOR

A gift to anyone who cares for the poor. Hal's life and work are emblematic of what can happen when we take seriously God's command to love our neighbor. We can all learn a lot from him.

—GABE AND REBEKAH LYONS, AUTHORS; FOUNDERS, Q IDEAS

I highly recommend this book from my friend and world-class-leader Hal Donaldson. Loaded with divine insight and compelling stories, it will inspire you to change your world and disrupt the status quo.

—MARIANO RIVERA, HALL OF FAME PITCHER, NEW YORK YANKEES

Speaks not only to changing the world on a grand scale; it's about what we can do in our daily lives to bring about change. Hal reminds us that our little bit matters. Inspiring and practical, one to refer to time and again.

—SANDRA STANLEY, NORTH POINT MINISTRIES

Drives home valuable principles through heartfelt, real-life stories. A manual for giving the right way and making your life count. You can't help shedding tears of joy as you read it, as it encourages you to give from the heart.

—CURT AND NANCY RICHARDSON, FOUNDERS, OTTER PRODUCTS

We each have a God-given duty in this world. Hal has inspired us to continue to ask ourselves what we are doing every single day to honor that duty. This book is the nudge we all need to motivate us into action.

—JONATHAN STEWART, PROFESSIONAL FOOTBALL PLAYER; PHILANTHROPIST; AND NATALIE STEWART, PHILANTHROPIST

Will fuel your faith, change your perspective, and give you keys for living out God's destiny for you. Hal's passion for life, unquenchable hope, and unshakable faith will spark a fire in you to change your world.

—DANNY GOKEY, RECORDING ARTIST; *AMERICAN IDOL* FINALIST

Disruptive Compassion is a call for us to expand our reach beyond church walls to people in need. Hal Donaldson tells us how.

—EARL SMITH, CHAPLAIN, GOLDEN STATE WARRIORS, SAN FRANCISCO 49ERS

It's easy to feel powerless and overwhelmed in a world of endless options and paths. A great tool to help narrow your focus on the identity, influence, and power God has called you to.

—VANCE MCDONALD, TIGHT END, PITTSBURGH STEELERS

There are not too many leaders I respect more than Hal Donaldson. I have experienced firsthand his generosity of a life filled with compassion. I'm so thankful for Hal, Convoy of Hope, and this incredible work.

—TYLER REAGIN, PRESIDENT, CATALYST

DISRUPTIVE
COMPASSION

DISRUPTIVE
COMPASSION

BECOMING THE REVOLUTIONARY
YOU WERE BORN TO BE

HAL DONALDSON

KIRK NOONAN & LINDSAY KAY DONALDSON

ZONDERVAN®

ZONDERVAN

Disruptive Compassion
Copyright © 2019 by Hal Donaldson, Kirk Noonan, and Lindsay Kay Donaldson

Requests for information should be addressed to:
Zondervan, *3900 Sparks Dr. SE, Grand Rapids, Michigan 49546*

ISBN 978-0-310-35530-4 (softcover)

ISBN 978-0-310-63314-3 (special edition)

ISBN 978-0-310-35532-8 (audio)

ISBN 978-0-310-35531-1 (ebook)

Author is represented by The Christopher Ferebee Agency, www.christopherferebee.com.

Cover design: James W. Hall IV
Cover illustration: baona/iStock
Interior design: Denise Froehlich

Printed in the United States of America

19 20 21 22 23 LSC 10 9 8 7 6 5 4 3 2 1

To Rick and Jan Britton and family.
Thank you for demonstrating the power
of kindness and compassion.

CONTENTS

FOREWORD

When I was young, I, like many young people, wanted to CHANGE THE WORLD. I didn't have any idea how I was going to do that, but that didn't matter. The world needed to be changed, and I would definitely be a part of that changing. I'm in my forties now, and I've seen many would-be world changers charge onto the scene, declare their intention, and then flame out, leaving the world unchanged or, in some cases, even a little bruised and battered by their brief but emphatic efforts. I'll confess I don't have much capacity anymore for loud young world changers and their grand declarations.

These days I'm so compelled by individuals of all ages who pick a problem to solve and solve it with a minimum of grand declarations. These days I've abandoned my own world-changer rally cry, and instead, each morning when I pray, I ask God to show me how to be helpful. That's the word these days: helpful. I'm more conscious than I've ever been of the brevity of life, and I want to end my life knowing that I helped in my own small way. That I gave more than I took, that I used what I was given, and that I played a long game, building something meaningful over time.

And that's why Hal Donaldson's life and story are so

profoundly moving to me. Honestly, if you go by the numbers, he has every reason to carry around a bullhorn and tell us how much world changing he's done: the good that Convoy of Hope has brought to the world is staggering, and I'm so thankful for it. And that great good has been done with humility, with a plan, and with a methodical, quiet faithfulness that I believe should guide each one of us as we seek to be helpful in this world.

This book is, in many ways, a compelling argument against many of the prevailing myths that haunt us. Some of us feel like our pasts—our wounds, the things we went without, the pain that shaped us—will define us forever. Hal experienced tragic loss and ongoing challenges, and instead of permitting those things to have the final word on the whole of his life, he allowed his experiences to yield empathy and gratitude. What an extraordinary and rare thing!

Some of us have bought into the myth that in order to achieve real success, what we build must be fast and flashy—two of the most corrosive and dangerous adjectives in our cultural language, I believe. Fast and flashy, whether applied to relief work, creative work, or used as markers of success, will never lead us toward durable, solid results. The restraint and patience that have marked Hal's leadership of Convoy of Hope present a compelling and timely alternative vision, one that values faithfulness and wisdom and long-range building over fast and flashy. What a necessary and inspiring story, one that has challenged me in so many ways.

—SHAUNA NIEQUIST

ACKNOWLEDGMENTS

Special thanks to Doree, Erin-Rae, Lauren, and Haly Donaldson. And deep appreciation to Janna, Kianna, Rhett, Nikolas, Barry, and Linda Noonan.

Thank you to everyone who has invested in and advocated and volunteered for expanding the reach of Convoy of Hope to the world's poor and suffering. This is *your* story. Through your commitment and support, you have made the world a better place.

INTRODUCTION

No more nukes! No more nukes!"

With fists raised, more than two thousand students chanted in the quad at San Jose State University. From the stage, activists shouted their demands while demonstrators waved hand-painted signs. Their energy rivaled that of a U2 concert.

I was just a spectator, but that didn't stop me from being jostled from all sides as protesters worked everyone into a frenzy.

"Bro, it's time to join the fight," a demonstrator proclaimed as he shoved a flyer in my hand.

I nodded but couldn't help but think, *This is a waste of time. The government doesn't give a rip what you and your pals think.*

Don't get me wrong, I believed in their right to protest and shared their fear of nuclear weapons. I just didn't see the point of squandering a ninety-degree day when we could have been soaking up rays on a beach in nearby Santa Cruz.

At the time, I didn't feel passionate enough about anything to join a protest. The way I saw it, God was in control of everything and the fate of the world rested in his hands, not mine. If he could deflect nuclear warheads with a flick of his finger, he didn't need my help. My time would be better spent slapping on sunscreen and catching some waves.

As far as I was concerned, a lot of protesters were wannabe rebels, troublemakers who exploited teenage rage for free weed, casual sex, and street cred. Sure, I admired their enthusiasm, but I just wanted to live my life my way and let someone else worry about injustice, politics, poverty, and pollution. I just wanted to become a sportswriter and be left alone to pursue my bucket list: a six-figure income, good health, a gorgeous wife, kids, a house in a gated community, and a beagle named Bo. I figured that wasn't too much to ask.

GUNS AND SPORTS

When I entered San Jose State University's school of journalism, my plan was to marry my love of sports with my passion for writing. I dreamed of watching baseball, basketball, and football games from the press box and being paid to write about them.

But those aspirations were dealt a blow when the editor of the *Spartan Daily* newspaper assigned me an editorial on gun control.

"I don't have a clue about gun control," I said. "I write sports."

"I don't give a [expletive] what you write!" snapped the editor. "Have it on my desk tomorrow—one thousand words."

"What's the angle?" I inquired.

"It's *your* editorial," he shot back, adding an F-bomb for punctuation.

If I thought the quad was bad, the newsroom was proving to be even more hardcore. It was a mosh pit of philosophies and lifestyles. Defending your position on politics, social issues, and religion wasn't optional. Occasionally, the debates were so fierce, the professors had to step into the ring and point students to neutral corners. I told myself, *I don't belong here. I just want to focus on sports.*

As I contemplated the editorial, reality smacked me in the face: no matter what position I took on gun control, I'd be dragged to the center of the ring and all my beliefs would be exposed. *Perfect, just how I wanted to kick off my college experience.*

It took two Snickers bars, a bag of Fritos, and three Mountain Dews, but I pulled an all-nighter and met the deadline.

Two days later, shaking with fear and from a caffeine overdose, I entered the newsroom to engage with fellow gladiators. Before the critique began, the editor approached my desk holding the morning newspaper. "Why the [expletive] are you writing sports? You should be writing more news—nice job."

"Thanks."

He took to the front of the newsroom and shouted, "Let's get started."

Typing came to an abrupt halt and phone calls ceased. Like synchronized swimmers, seventy-five heads snapped toward the editor and our three ninja-assassin professors. Article by article, they shredded our work and invited cutting student feedback. I suddenly felt like an MMA fighter entering the octagon: throat constricting, palms sweating, veins bulging.

"Okay, let's go to the editorial on gun control," said one of the middle-aged ninjas. "This one will make some readers mad, but we're in the business of making people think, aren't we?"

Gulp.

The professor continued. "I thought the lead and quotes were strong. But it could have used more statistics to help the reader understand the issue. Overall, it's a solid piece. Other opinions?"

The editor at the city desk piped in. "I don't agree with all his points," she said, "but it's well constructed."

"Any other comments?" asked the professor.

Crickets.

Awesome, I cheered to myself, *I survived without a black eye or bruised ego.*

But my celebration was short lived. A student with a harsh-is-putting-it-mildly reputation raised her hand. "The writing wasn't tight enough for me. The fourth and fifth paragraphs are worthless and the final paragraph left me hanging. B-minus at best."

"Ouch," I whispered to the student seated next to me, who subtly leaned away as if to say, "I'm not with this guy."

Her comments were all it took. The avalanche began and a twenty-minute discussion ensued. I nodded occasionally to make everyone think I was taking their words to heart. But my mind was elsewhere. It was a strange setting for a confessional, but as the debate droned on, I told myself the truth: *For years, I've said that living out my dreams was enough. That's a lie. I say I don't care about social issues. That's also a lie. I pretend for one simple reason: I feel inferior and I'm insecure. I'm just a fatherless welfare kid who doesn't have the confidence to stand up for what he believes. Fear of rejection and ridicule have muted my voice and relegated me to a bystander. There's no denying it—I'm writing sports because it's a distraction. It helps me escape the horrors of the real world two hours at a time. When the game clock starts, it's as if politics, human suffering, injustice, and crime don't exist. In that moment, the game is all that matters. For me, it's a safe place in an angry world.*

My self-analysis was interrupted by a question from the professor. "Hal, any reaction to the comments you've heard today?"

Crickets.

Awkwardly, I blurted, "Thank you—real helpful."

I tried to sound sincere, but the professor wasn't buying it.

He tossed me a dissatisfied look. "What specifically did you find helpful?"

"All of it," I said through lying teeth.

Yeah, he definitely didn't buy it.

When the ninjas finally turned to critiquing other students, I felt like racing out the door and splashing cold water on my face. Instead, I retreated to my thoughts. But even there I couldn't escape the truth: I had become proficient at denying and deflecting social responsibility. I was the guy who walked across the street to avoid a homeless person, the one who sat back and did nothing when another kid was being bullied. I told myself I couldn't make a difference anyway, but that wasn't true. I was just another coward using cynicism as a shield. It was time to decide what kind of life I really wanted. Was I content to watch the world from the comfort of a press box, or did I want to risk injury by playing in the game? What was more important? Comfort and security or fulfillment and purpose? It was time to answer that question once and for all.

DR. NO

One of my journalism professors was dubbed Dr. No. Whenever a student posed a trivial question in a mock interview, he'd bark, "No, no, no—if you don't ask the right question, you'll never get the right answer."

With him, it was never just "no." It was always "no, no, no."

During one of his workshops, he said, "One question must be asked in every interview. It's the *why* question. If you don't ask why, you're failing the reader and you're going to fail my class. You have a duty to dig until you find the truth."

I knew Dr. No was trying to prepare us for the real world. But I had no desire to dig up dirt or volunteer for covert missions. I wasn't destined for the *National Enquirer*, and I definitely wasn't signing up for the CIA.

The truth is I didn't want to confront anyone with the *why* question, not even God or myself. It was easier to dodge social responsibility and avoid conflict if I kept my distance and kept my mouth shut.

As the days wore on, my editor's words haunted me: "Why are you writing sports? You need to be writing more news." I was torn. Writing sports came easy, but writing hard news would put me in the game. If I ditched my sports journalism dreams and began writing *news* news, I knew what it would mean. (And that's what I was afraid of.) Like the students in the quad, I'd have to become a citizen of the world and assume some responsibility for its problems. I'd have to contribute something with more impact than sports features. I'd have to start asking the *why* question.

Whether it was God or my conscience speaking to me, I knew what I had to do; I asked the editor to transfer me from the sports beat to the news pages. I went from covering championships and knee injuries to writing about corruption and injustice. I assumed I was setting out to become a hard-nosed investigative journalist. Little did I know that this decision—and the quest for the life I really wanted—was the beginning of my journey to become the revolutionary I was born to be.

Let me fast-forward past my days at San Jose State and share a few things I've learned since then. That will lend context to some ideas that could transform the way you view yourself, your circumstances, and your future.

First, every movement begins with revolutionaries who grow disillusioned with how things are and imagine how things could be. They possess the heart of a liberator. They deliver speeches and write manifestos daring others to ask themselves and others, "Why?" They inspire others to dream of a better future and challenge them to make sacrifices for the sake of lasting change. Revolutionaries remind others that movements begin in *their* hearts and minds. Because it's only then that they, collectively, can change the status quo. In other words, movements start small. They start with you.

You might be saying, "Hey, I want to help change the world, but I don't want to be called a revolutionary." Perhaps the word conjures images of soldiers crawling through the jungles of South America or fist-pumping rebels marching through the streets. But that's a different kind of revolutionary. The ones referred to in this book lead with kindness. They are a force for good in a world crying out for hope and mercy. The label you wear isn't important. You may feel more comfortable being called an advocate, a social worker, a champion, or a concerned citizen. But the word *revolutionary* seems to fit the magnitude of the problem. The world doesn't need tweaking. It needs profound change. It needs a revolution marked by disruptive compassion.

You don't have to be a politician or public speaker to spark a revolution. You can be a schoolteacher, singer, secretary, supervisor, or salesperson. You possess the power to provoke change and rally people to a united act of compassion.

But the truth is, words are not enough.

Even though movements begin with questions born of dissatisfaction, they are fueled by people who step out and do something. It's not enough to complain or criticize. Your words and passion may fire people up, but seldom does that lead to solutions. You must act.

Taking action means taking that intimidating first step. It means leaping over uncertainty, reluctance, and fear. You're not alone. Every revolutionary must conquer doubt and feelings of inadequacy. But you'll discover that the first step is often the most rewarding. It's the one you'll remember forever. It's the day you said to yourself, "I don't know exactly where my heart is leading me, but I'm going for it."

Someone said, "The two greatest days in your life are the day you were born and the day you find out why."[1] Hopefully this book will help you discover what you were born to do and equip you to confront the status quo through disruptive compassion. Disruption is an interruption to the normal course. You can be that interruption, and this book will show you how. If people like you don't stand up, the normal course will only perpetuate more oppression, racism, poverty, war, death, and decay. The world needs revolutionaries who are tired of seeing hatred spread and love retreat. Will you stand alongside millions and declare, "Enough is enough. That's unacceptable. I'm ready to do my part to change the world"?

I know, "change the world" sounds like a campaign slogan. Every activist, politician, and churchgoer uses the phrase. We've heard it repeated until we no longer believe it's achievable. After all, most people are more inclined to talk about it than work for it. Sure, the phrase gives us hope. It makes us feel better. But what does it really mean? In this book, *change the world* denotes a direction rather than a destination. It doesn't mean you can solve every problem and rid the world of every injustice. (Leave that to the superheroes.) This book is about finding fulfillment by accepting your God-given duty to the world. It's about making changes in your life and driving in the right direction so that one day you can pass the keys to the next generation and not have to apologize for the condition of the car.

AGITATORS

Today's revolutionaries are compassionate agitators. They stir things up. Ask tough questions. Even risk ridicule and rejection. Because they get it. The days of sitting back and watching the world deteriorate are over. Silence and inaction only prolong the problems. It's time to move beyond pity, anger, and disgust and do something to disrupt the status quo. It's time to face your fears and doubts and take the first step toward action.

Former US Congressman Tony Hall (D-Ohio) was viewed by some as an "agitator" who challenged the status quo, but he really became a revolutionary following a trip to famine-plagued Ethiopia. There, despite the heroic efforts of relief workers, he saw children die of malnutrition and dehydration. When he returned to the US, he authored emergency legislation to increase aid. But when Congress voted to eliminate his House Committee on Hunger (the only committee focused on hunger), he refused to remain silent and took a courageous first step: he embarked on a highly publicized twenty-two-day hunger strike. Instead of donning his tuxedo to attend five-thousand-dollar-a-plate dinners and carrying on with business as usual, Tony refused to eat until Congress paid attention. Before long, students from two hundred universities and five thousand high schools joined him in the protest. And together they pressured Congress into restoring the committee. Tony's disruption even led to the World Bank donating $100 million to the fight against world hunger. Because of his passion and courage, Tony was later appointed ambassador to the United Nations Agencies for Food and Agriculture. His protest is a shining example of what can happen when we reject the status quo and refuse to back down.

Throughout history, revolutionaries have conquered their fears and stepped out. Activist-preacher Charles Finney used his voice to abolish slavery. British citizen George Williams founded the YMCA in protest of child labor. William and Catherine Booth started the Salvation Army to rescue the homeless and feed the hungry. Clara Barton was a nurse in the American Civil War before she founded the American Red Cross to help those affected by disasters. Nelson Mandela broke the back of apartheid in South Africa. And Martin Luther King Jr. led peaceful demonstrations for racial equality. Each one identified a problem, took action, and produced lasting change.

The greatest protester the world has ever known is Jesus. He didn't march, picket, or boycott, yet his fingerprints can still be seen on movements all over the world. Dissatisfied with conditions on earth, he launched a movement of disruptive compassion. Without resorting to violence or verbal assault, he led a resistance to oppression, prejudice, religious elitism, and hatred. He said, "Love your neighbor as yourself," "Be kind to your enemies," and "Protect the weak." Countercultural, to say the least. He went beyond words, too, by feeding the hungry, healing the sick, and befriending beggars, prostitutes, and outcasts. His message was radical for his time, and his acts of compassion were misunderstood by many, but that didn't stop him. Power brokers feared he secretly sought to topple governments and religious institutions, but he had a much greater purpose. He came to disrupt the status quo and give people hope through love and compassion.

Regardless of your view of Jesus, the principles he championed are timeless. He created a model that revolutionaries have followed for two thousand years. And it's those same principles that guided my journey and can direct yours too. The world is desperate for people who are willing to lay everything on the line to make our home a better place. Wars, injustice, racism, famine, and poverty have left their scars, but there's still hope if revolutionaries like you practice disruptive compassion.

SANITIZING THE WORLD?

Disruptive compassion is not code for sanitizing the world or condemning people who don't measure up to your standards. Jesus never taught that. He led with grace and mercy, not judgment. He refused to isolate himself from those society considered unholy or unclean. He never said, "Go unto all the earth with thy pail of Lysol and scrubbeth every corner of thy globe." No, disruptive compassion is not a mission to decontaminate people. It's not an excuse to clean up those deemed dirty or lowly.

Instead, it's a declaration that every person is valued and loved just as they are. It's a conviction that people shouldn't have to be malnourished. The sick shouldn't have to die. The abused shouldn't have to suffer. Disruptive compassion is a rejection of the status quo and a belief that a tidal wave of love and acts of kindness can heal a wounded world.

This is not a superficial game, with token deeds to make us feel good. To change the world, disruptive compassion has to go deep. It requires new priorities, values, and logic. It means a radical commitment to the Golden Rule: "Do for others what you want them to do for you."[2] The tide of hatred and racism will not be stemmed by more hatred. Tyranny will not turn to peace because of violent protests. Corporations will not exercise social responsibility because of insincere boycotts. Criminals will not be brought to justice with empty petitions. Social change begins with people like you disrupting their lives and choosing to make each day a relentless demonstration of love, respect, and sacrifice.

You want to change the world? The common advice is to "jump out of the recliner and do the next kind thing in front of you!" Maybe you find yourself feeling like I did for years—paralyzed by fear because I didn't believe I could make a difference. I had resigned myself to watching poverty, racism, human trafficking, and crime play out on the world's IMAX screen. I felt powerless and insignificant. I didn't know what to do, and I didn't have the confidence to try. If that sounds like you, I pray this book is your road map to greater influence in a world that needs your voice.

My diploma from San Jose State University reads "Bachelors of Arts: Journalism," but my education went far beyond developing writing and reporting skills. By the time I graduated, I was equipped to speak for myself and stand up for others. But my university experience was just the beginning of a journey that took me from my back yard to urban war zones in the United States and refugee camps in Africa, from natural disasters in Haiti to safe houses in India. Those life-and-death experiences, chronicled in this book, led to the founding of an international relief organization known as

Convoy of Hope, which has served more than one hundred fifteen million people through hunger relief, jobs training for mothers, agricultural initiatives, community outreach and training, and disaster response. Along the way, I learned that anything is possible if you let disruptive compassion fuel you.

As you read this book and embark on your own journey, ask yourself this bottom-line question: What's holding you back from becoming the revolutionary you were born to be? What needs to happen in your life for you to establish new priorities and shape new disciplines? This is your moment. The world needs you. Read on and discover how to spark a movement that really can change the world.

CHAPTER 1

BELIEVE

It doesn't matter where you come from, what you have or don't have, what you lack, or what you have too much of. But all you need to have is faith in God, an undying passion for what you do and what you choose to do in this life, and a relentless drive and the will to do whatever it takes to be successful in whatever you put your mind to.

—Stephen Curry

It was a drizzly night in Detroit, Michigan—moonless and foreboding. Having graduated from college and now working as a journalist, I had flown to the Motor City to report on the city's economic crisis. But, privately, my editor said, "Downtown Detroit's becoming a war zone—find out what's going on." Knowing the city's reputation, I recruited two buddies as backup for the trip. That first night we drove into a borough where prostitutes mingled with gangbangers like housewives do with their neighbors in the suburbs. The windshield wipers on the rental car squeaked in sync with the radio as we neared a tiny, dilapidated hotel. A neon sign directed customers to the front door, and a number of scantily clad girls paraded in and out with their dates. We walked into the hotel's lobby hoping to land an interview.

Flickering fluorescent lights hung above the cramped lobby. They gave everything a bluish hue, including the gaunt-faced man with dark stubble who manned the counter. A cigarette drooped from the corner of his mouth, and he reeked of body odor.

Like an overeager salesman, I launched into my pitch, telling him we wanted to interview some of his girls.

"You cops?" he grumbled.

"No," I defended. "Just gathering some stories."

"For what?"

"I'm a journalist."

"What d'ya want?"

"Writing a magazine article about the city—no names."

"Not interested," he said, scanning the stacks of rumpled papers and large ashtray brimming with cigarette butts on the counter.

I persisted. "Let me talk to just one girl—fifteen minutes."

"I ain't got time for this. Either you want a room or you don't," he said, cursing under his breath.

"I'll take a room—one hour."

My buddies shot me a nervous glance as I slapped a twenty on the counter.

Key in hand, we maneuvered up the stairs. Room 28 had a lot of stories to tell. It had the stench of smoke, scratched brass doorknobs, and soiled carpet. The bed was covered with a thin orange bedspread bearing numerous stains and cigarette burns. In the corner was a broken television, and the curtains were tacked to the wall.

Without a knock, a girl appeared in the doorway and leaned in. A taller girl peered over her shoulder. Both wore tight skirts, fishnet stockings, and long earrings.

"You police?" the girl asked.

I shook my head. "Reporters from out of town."

"Which of us do you want?" the first girl asked. "Depends what you're into."

"We just want to talk with you," I said.

"What for?" the other girl asked.

"We're doing a story for a magazine—won't use your names or anything," I said. "Twenty bucks for fifteen minutes of your time."

"Twenty each," the first girl demanded.

I nodded.

They weren't runway models and they looked older than their professed ages—twenty-two and twenty-four. Their hair was coarse, their eyes lifeless. I thought, *It's hard to believe they were once little girls who played games and climbed trees. Now they're playthings for strangers who don't even bother to ask their names.*

The girls puffed on cigarettes as they described their lives: abuse, STDs, and unwanted pregnancies. Many sold their bodies for drugs. Theirs was a cycle of despair that played out every night in makeshift brothels around the world.

"Why do you do this?" I asked naively. "There are better things out there for you."

"I'd love to escape this hell," the taller girl said. "Just don't know how." She took a long drag on her cigarette, then stared at the wall as if wishing she were somewhere else.

"Time's up," the first girl said, bouncing off the bed and bolting for the door. Reluctantly, the taller girl followed.

The door slammed and I said what all three of us were thinking: "Guys, without a miracle, those girls will be dead before they're thirty. And the sad thing is no one will care or even notice. Because no one believes they can do anything about it—not even me."

Change the world? That's an absolute joke if you don't believe in your mission. Seriously, ask yourself if you believe a "better world" is possible. Do you really believe you can play a role in reducing poverty, pollution, abuse, racism, crime, human trafficking, and more? If so, this book will help guide you forward.

Guy Kawasaki worked alongside Apple founder Steve Jobs and spoke about the power of belief: "What I learned from Steve Jobs is . . . you need to foster the belief in what you are dreaming so that it becomes a reality. Which is very different than saying I don't expect anybody to believe it until I see it. You need people to believe it before they can see it."[1]

The true enemies of progress are doubt, apathy, and blame. They must be conquered in your mind (that is the first battleground) before you can become the revolutionary you were born to be.

DOUBT

I descended into the dark labyrinth of tunnels beneath Moscow, Russia. Young girls lined the walls like mannequins in a department store window as lustful men paraded by like Saturday evening shoppers. I stood in this dungeon of sorts and watched as customers made their selections and negotiated prices. Although the setting had changed, I felt the same disgust and sadness as months earlier in Detroit. From nowhere, a young girl brushed up next to me. She smiled seductively and spoke in Russian. I couldn't understand her words, but I knew her question. When I shook my head no, she turned to another patron twice her age. Not even Hollywood could glamorize this storyline. The girls were riding a carousel of abuse—business as usual in Moscow's underground.

At that moment, I felt completely powerless. Realistically, what could I do to rescue them and bring the ringleaders to justice? Nothing—absolutely nothing.

Powerlessness is doubting one's ability to bring change. It's doubting that transformation is even possible, because, if we're honest, we haven't seen enough of it. You may also feel helpless because you've been told "you can't do anything." Perhaps you've been belittled and beaten down to the point you don't believe in yourself. If you're alone right now, yell, "I *can* do it!" (I wouldn't advise that if you're reading this in a crowded train or coffee shop.) Sure, massive injustices and social problems exist that you can't fix on your own. Nobody can. But that fact has nothing to do with your ability, identity, or value. It has nothing to do with your being smart enough, good enough, famous enough, or powerful enough. It just means some problems require an entire regiment of revolutionaries to move the needle.

It's up to you to reject the lies that keep you down and render you ineffective. Rather than fixating on what can't be done, focus on the things you can do. Perhaps the simplest of those is love. "Love each other as if your life depended on it. Love makes up for practically anything. Be quick to give a meal to the hungry, a bed to the homeless—cheerfully. Be generous with the different things God gave you" (1 Peter 4:8–10 MSG).

Without risking my life or banishment to a Siberian labor camp, I had no way to rescue those girls in Detroit or Moscow. But, despite my limitations, I was far from powerless. Nothing was stopping me, for example, from assisting an organization committed to helping young women escape slavery and prostitution. When our belief in a mission is stronger than our doubt in ourselves, we will find ways to contribute to the cause.

"Apathy can be overcome by enthusiasm, and enthusiasm can only be aroused by . . . an ideal, which takes the imagination by storm, and second, by a definite intelligible plan for carrying that ideal into practice," said British historian Arnold J. Toynbee.[2] In other words, actions give credibility and life to our words.

It's impossible to muster enthusiasm for change if you believe every condition and event in the world is inevitable and we're merely robots at the mercy of a Cosmic Programmer. Your hope will eventually disintegrate if you don't believe your choices and actions can influence the future.

APATHY

Helen Keller said, "We may have found a cure for most evils; but we have found no remedy for the worst of them all, the apathy of human beings."[3] Apathy is a disease that attacks the nervous system. It dulls emotions and dams tears. And ultimately it leaves the world with fewer voices to speak out against injustice, oppression, and abuse.

There's no magic pill to make us care about the state of the world. For revolutionaries, that begins with a basic understanding that whatever happens to others impacts them too. The health and happiness of others is connected to the well-being of the world. We're all connected.

When a father tucked his eight-year-old daughter into bed, he asked her a serious question: "What's the one thing you're looking forward to the most about heaven?" Immediately, the girl's eyes lit up and she exclaimed, "I can't wait for big roller coasters with no waiting lines!" It was apparent she'd already thought long and hard about the prospect. "I also want to slide down rainbows and have picnics on the clouds," she said.

"Do you want any pets?" the father asked.

She nodded emphatically. "I want my own dinosaur."

You can appreciate the child's enthusiasm, but some adults are so eager for heaven that they've turned a blind eye to the needs on earth. Heaven isn't a hall pass. It isn't an excuse for inaction here. You weren't placed on this planet to bide your time in comfort while others suffer. It's impossible to love God and hate the world. If you love God, you also despise hunger, injustice, poverty, racism, abuse, human trafficking, and more. If he hasn't given up on the world, why should you? Your God-given choices today shape the world others live in tomorrow. "If anyone thinks he is religious and does not bridle his tongue but deceives his heart, this person's religion is worthless. Religion that is pure and undefiled . . . is this: to visit orphans and widows in their affliction" (James 1:26–27 ESV).

Apathy is telling yourself, *The most important thing is that I make it through to the other side—what happens to everyone else is their business.* It's saying, *Change is impossible or inevitable no matter what I do, so why should I get involved?*

Author Allen Tappe said, "Change will happen whether

you like it or not. Positive change, however, requires choice. You can choose to accept natural change or you can choose to fight it. . . . The power to choose is yours. The responsibility for choice is yours. You have no one else to blame for the way you choose to respond to life. It is your deal."[4]

I learned this firsthand in Belfast, Northern Ireland.

It was Friday night and bar patrons spilled into the streets. For the long-standing cultural war between Protestants and Catholics, alcohol is akin to jet fuel. What began with name-calling erupted into a drunken and bloody brawl. But that's what residents expect in Belfast: short fuses and long conflicts. With recorder in hand, I set out to interview some of the combatants. It didn't take me long to understand the value of the "Peace Wall" that bisects the city. The two factions hate one another but sometimes struggle to explain why. One college student said, "My brother was killed by an assassin. I'm going to spend the rest of my life getting even."

I was there to write an objective article, giving equal coverage to both sides. But when a militant group learned I was an American journalist, they invited me to attend their protest. Hours later, I found myself in the middle of an angry mob, marching elbow-to-elbow with the group's president.

I asked, "What do you want Americans to know about your cause?"

"That we will not give up," he snapped.

"Do you advocate violence?" I asked.

"We uphold the right of the Irish people to engage in controlled and disciplined force," he said.

"Do you fear for your life?"

"That's not important—I'm more concerned about getting the job done. Thank you," he said, breaking off the interview.

I didn't fully understand the factions or issues dividing them, but it was obvious everyone was weary of the struggle. The same movie—with the same ending—was replayed year after year. Many had lost hope that anything would change. Rather than writing a new script, they'd become accustomed to reruns.

You too were created to be a screenwriter—not a mere moviegoer. You were destined to participate in the inventive process. Throwing up your hands and saying, "Whatever happens—happens," is akin to saying, "This is someone else's movie—not mine." Start writing and believing that you can write a different story for a world in need.

Apathy gets blamed for everything that's wrong in the world. Why malnutrition? Apathy. Why pollution and waste? Apathy. Why political disengagement? Apathy. It's become a tired cliché. But perhaps many are emotionally and intellectually detached because they've chosen "intentional ignorance." They don't want to know about the underbelly of prostitution, drugs, and prejudice, for example. Because once they know, they feel guilty for not doing something to change it. It's just easier to look the other way or pretend they don't hear the cries for help. The Bible says, "When you happen on someone who's in trouble or needs help among your people . . . don't look the other way pretending you don't see him" (Deut. 15:7 MSG). Make no mistake, we've all done that—no one can point fingers. But when we take deliberate steps to avoid someone in need, we really don't care.

Martin Luther King Jr. said, "Nothing in all the world is more dangerous than sincere ignorance and conscientious stupidity." In other words, ignorance is just another form of apathy. It leads to inaction and silence and preserves the status quo. We don't protest what we don't know about, and we don't defend those we can't see. It's as if the world is busy dancing to a house DJ while an adjacent room is on fire with people trapped inside. We dismiss the hint of smoke as the music plays on. Of course, if we saw them, we'd take action. If we knew them, we'd run for help. But because no flames are visible, we don't bother to sound the alarm.

In 1965 Billy Graham wrote a bestselling book titled *World on Fire*. In it, he wrote, "Mr. Average Man is comfortable in his complacency and as unconcerned as a silverfish ensconced in a carton of discarded magazines on world affairs. Man is not asking any questions, because his social benefits from the government give him a false security. This is his trouble and his tragedy. Modern man has become a spectator of world events, observing on his television screen without becoming involved. He watches the ominous events of our times pass before his eyes, while he sips his beer in a comfortable chair. He does not seem to realize what is happening to him. He does not understand that his world is on fire and that he is about to be burned with it."[5]

Intentional ignorance that leads to disconnectedness and silence has cost millions of lives. In Jerusalem, at Yad Vashem: The World Holocaust Remembrance Center, hang graphic photographs of concentration camps, gas chambers, and death trains. The images left me horrified and ashamed to be a part of the human race. As I listened to the audio descriptions of survivors, I couldn't help but ask how the world allowed this to happen. How could nations ignore genocide? Families were ripped apart and millions of Jewish citizens were executed. Meanwhile the world collectively put its hands over its eyes and said nothing.

"The biggest mistake that was made during the Holocaust was that people didn't speak up," said Holocaust survivor Sonia K. "The Holocaust took place because individuals, groups, and nations made decisions to act or not to act. The world was quiet then, but we must not be quiet again. Now we know better. We must all commit to making the world a better, kinder, and more understanding place. Perhaps it's as simple as speaking out when you see something wrong and saying, 'I know better.' But please, never be a bystander."[6]

During the civil rights movement, Dr. King said, "In the end, we will remember not the words of our enemies but the silence of our friends."[7]

The price of silence was witnessed in Flint, Michigan. The city's water problem was first raised in 2014. But it was largely ignored by officials and compounded by head-scratching decisions. In 2015, they claimed the problem was under control. A year later, they declared a state of emergency. By that time, thousands of children had already been exposed to high levels of toxins in their drinking water. Because of incompetence or apathy, thousands of Flint's poorest citizens suffered the consequences.

Natasha Puri wrote, "We encounter pictures and videos that truly expose us to these events, but rather than taking the pictures, we should be changing them. These instances should not be viewed as headlines; they are catalysts for change. And if we're not doing anything to resolve them, then we're also part of the problem. . . . Apathy is more than just indifference; it's an attitude we need to abandon. There seems to be some propensity to wait for someone else to act and take initiative."[8]

When the public learned the magnitude of the Flint water crisis, television pundits and human rights leaders were outraged. To their credit, CNN went beyond debate and took action. The television network contacted Convoy of Hope to help them distribute 500,000 bottles of water to Flint residents. Dozens of volunteers from the network were on hand, including commentators Don Lemon, Van Jones, and Donna Brazile. In the weeks that followed, CNN and Nestlé Waters North America provided an additional twelve truckloads of water to be distributed by local churches and groups. In all, Convoy of Hope and its partners distributed four hundred tractor trailers of water to families in need. Together, these groups and organizations rejected apathy and said, "We must do something."

BLAME

Admittedly I was looking for someone to blame when my daughter, Lindsay, and I walked the streets of Mumbai, India. There, the homeless are deposited throughout the city, sleeping on mats and patches of dirt. But even the homeless are more fortunate than the thousands of women and girls victimized by traffickers. Some as young as eight spend their days and nights lining Falkland Road, the beating heart of the red light district, wearing heavy makeup and colorful saris to attract customers. Although many were born into the industry, countless others are kidnapped or knowingly sold into slavery by family members. The experience was darker and the sights more evil than we had expected. Can one really prepare to see such human exploitation on a single block? The first glimmer of hope didn't come until we visited a safe house founded by Project Rescue, an organization that combats human trafficking. There, women and girls receive counseling and job training in a protected community. One woman shared her story of abuse and a harrowing escape. Then she looked me in the eye and said, "The suffering will continue unless people like you do something." I knew she was right, but often it's easier to curse the darkness and blame someone else.

Sometimes we blame our inaction on our inability to see immediate results. For example, have you ever rescued a friend in financial trouble and a few weeks later he or she was back asking for more? Or have you donated to a charity and discovered they were overpromising and underdelivering? You probably said to yourself, *I did my part—next time it's someone else's turn.* That's the natural reaction, because we're emotionally programmed for results. When we don't see the outcome we anticipate, we're tempted to throw in the towel. Our trust was broken and time and resources wasted. But there is another option. Rather than walking away altogether, what about partnering with someone else? Just because one person or group failed you doesn't mean another will. Don't let your passion for a cause wane because you have someone to blame. Doing something with a new partner is better than doing nothing.

It was a dinner party I'll never forget. I dropped in on a friend at work and he invited me to grab chicken wings with him and his coworkers. In a matter of minutes, we formed an impressive pyramid of discarded chicken bones in the center of the table. All eight of us had sauce up to our elbows. For two hours, I eavesdropped on their conversation. They blamed politicians, the news media, corporations, governments, and criminals for the perilous state of the world. "If there's a God, I think he gave up on us a long time ago," a young man said with a shake of his head. Another piped in: "Nothing is going to change until they start putting people in jail and taking their money." The men nodded in agreement. At the end of the table, a man with a raspy voice said, "The world is going to hell and there's nothing we can do about it."

I didn't want to intrude on their "therapy" session—but talk about depressing! I felt like distributing party hats and kazoos and dropping balloons from the ceiling.

I was conspicuously quiet until the person seated next to me asked, "So what do you think about all the crap going on in this country?"

I glanced at my friend across the table, who rolled his eyes.

"Yeah, well, I guess I still believe things can get better if we—"

He interrupted me with a slap on the back. "Good for you—pass my *hopeful* friend some more wings."

While I nibbled, they resumed their pity party. I stayed for the duration, feeling like I had crashed their club meeting. Evidently pessimism was a prerequisite for membership.

It's easy to fixate on the negative and assign blame. But that's neither healthy nor productive. Over the course of that dinner, what changed? Did anyone learn something valuable about the situations being discussed? Were any viewpoints challenged or solutions offered? No—nothing. In contrast, I've found that revolutionaries spend more time seeking solutions than casting blame.

Perhaps you rejected apathy a long time ago. And you already believe you can help stem the tide of injustice, oppression, and poverty. But you're confronted with a mounting challenge. You find yourself driven by pressure rather than passion. The pressures to perform, earn a living, and achieve guide your decisions. Deep down, you'd prefer to be led by passion, but you feel entrapped by goals, expectations, and responsibilities. If that describes you, step back and just get real with yourself. Nothing is gained by beating yourself up for not doing more. No one expects you to quit your job so you can run an orphanage in the mountains of Haiti, for example. Just do all you can with what you have now. And stop blaming yourself.

I learned as much after a ride-along with the Chicago Police Department. The midnight shift was more than I bargained for. As soon as we left the precinct, I entered a world far removed from suburbia. In the first hour, when the police officer stepped away, he left me alone with a gang member who didn't hide his disdain for law enforcement.

"Gangbangers like me hate cops," he said with a scowl. I noted his colorful tattoos and fiery eyes. He was ready to fight. "I've always been in gangs, man. It's all I know."

"What's the gang into?" I asked.

He smirked and shook his head. "Just good law-abidin' citizens."

It took me a while to get beyond his act, but his attitude changed abruptly and his tone softened as he spoke about his childhood and the day his father checked out. "Everything fell on my mother and grandmother," he said. "They worked extra jobs to feed us, but it wasn't always enough. I helped the only way I could—workin' for the gang."

I nodded. I had heard this story before.

He snapped back into character, saying, "Man, it ain't a bad life—easy money and lots of girls."

"You ever worry about another gang taking you out?"

"Nah—I got my brothers watchin' me."

"You think you'll ever leave the gang?"

"It's family—you don't leave family."

When he spotted the policeman, he turned and walked the other way.

Both of us knew the pain of tragedy, but we had chosen to take different trails. He was swallowed by anger; I was cradled in love. After my father died, his best friend, Bill Davis, stepped into the chaos and redirected my life with grace, sacrifice, and acceptance. He said, "Hal, don't allow the tragedy of your childhood to become a lifelong excuse, because where you start in life doesn't have to dictate where you end." Yoda himself couldn't have said it any better.

What if this kid had a Bill Davis in his life? I said to myself. *Chances are he wouldn't be in a gang dodging bullets and prison sentences.*

Too many underestimate the power of their words, presence, and acts of kindness. Even when given in small doses for short durations, you can change the trajectory of a person's life. Don't surrender to excuses or give in to lies. Instead, reject apathy and believe that you *can* change someone's world.

Ask yourself right now, "What lies have I listened to that are preventing me from becoming everything the world needs me to be?"

CHAPTER 2

DEFINE THE MISSION

I read this poem that I loved at my high school graduation speech about what a successful life was to me. And it's to know that one life has breathed easier because you've lived. To me, that's success.

—Melinda Gates

Zombie phobia kicked in as I climbed the hospital's dimly lit cement steps. For some reason, every hospital scene in every zombie movie I'd ever seen came flooding back. But this was no ordinary hospital or hospice. It was Mother Teresa's Home for Dying Destitutes in Kolkata, India.

I had arrived in the city just twenty-four hours earlier to write a book on legendary missionaries Mark and Huldah Buntain. They had arranged for me to interview Mother Teresa—the chance of a lifetime. I wasn't sure what to expect, but I'd heard stories of her work my entire life. I guess I imagined she had a halo over her head. I said to myself, *I'm just a kid—I don't know the proper etiquette. Am I supposed to bow, shake hands, or kiss her cheek?* Trying the latter seemed risky, so I decided to wing it and follow her lead.

Garbed in her distinctive white and blue sari, she shuffled to a bench. Smiling, she asked, "What's your name, young man?"

Several beats passed before I could respond. "Hal Donaldson."

"Where are you from and what do you do?" she asked.

"I'm a writer from the United States. I came to Kolkata to write a book on Mark and Huldah Buntain."

Her face seemed to light up. "They have helped many in our city."

"Yes, they have big hearts. May I ask you a few questions?"

She nodded. "If it will help them and their work."

For the next twenty minutes, I scribbled her quotes in my reporter's notebook, trying not to miss one detail. As I wrote I thought, *I feel like I'm talking to my grandmother—without the milk and cookies—rather than a recipient of the Nobel Peace Prize.* Repeatedly she deflected my praises. "It's all because of God," she said.

As our time came to a close, she leaned forward. "Young man, can I ask what you do to help the poor?"

Her question wasn't accusative, demanding, or condescending. It was just a question. But to me it felt laced with expectation. If I lied to Mother Teresa, I was surely putting my life in jeopardy. So I told the truth. I glanced away and said, "I'm really not doing anything."

She could have condemned me, chastised me, or struck me with a lightsaber and I wouldn't have blamed her. Instead, she smiled and said, "Everyone can do something."

Internally I launched into protest: *I feel enough shame already. Take away my milk and cookie privileges. Or ask God to give me a cavity or two. But please, no more guilt trips.*

Little did she know how devastated I was by the sight of children living in tiny hovels, lapping water from streams filled with sewage, and climbing atop garbage heaps. I was new to this scale of poverty, and my emotions were being squeezed. Meanwhile, I was staying at the opulent Oberoi Grand Hotel. I had never seen such a display of marble tile, brilliant brass fixtures, ornate pottery, and crystal chandeliers. Nightly, from the safety of that luxurious room, I heard the cries of hunger and moans of disease from Kolkata's homeless population outside my window. I tossed and turned in the plushest of beds. I wish I could say sleep eluded me because I was asking, "How can I help them?" But in reality I was plagued by a very different question: "Now that I know, how can I carry on with my life the same way?"

I visited Kolkata prior to the present government's rise to power. Since then, India has made great strides and become an economic force. In the 1940s, Kolkata was decimated by famine and disease. So, in response, Mother Teresa and the Buntains started feeding programs, medical clinics, and schools. They defined their mission and, despite adversity and great risk, pressed on to meet their objectives.

As with them, sometimes your circumstances determine your mission. In other words, sometimes you don't have to go looking for your mission—the mission finds you. Mother Teresa came to Kolkata as a teacher and headmistress at a school. The Buntains came to the city as missionaries to establish a church. When confronted with poverty, disease, and illiteracy, they didn't throw up their hands and say, "It's someone else's problem." They didn't curse the darkness and walk away. They took action. The first (and most important) steps to accomplishing a mission are to recognize a need and accept responsibility for doing something about it.

Trekking across a schoolyard with Mark Buntain was like accompanying a rock star through a crowded arena. Children dashed toward him, clamoring for a hug or a pat on the head. He greeted each one by name and offered them snacks from his pocket.

"Do you ever get tired of this?" I asked.

"No, they're our mission. They're why we're here."

"Do you ever feel like you've given up a normal life? I know you've sacrificed a lot."

I struck a nerve with that question. He turned and locked eyes with me. "This isn't sacrifice—this is a privilege."

Hours later, I sat alone in my hotel room, fending off tears, confusion, and shame. I felt like swearing at the world and punching the walls until my knuckles were bloody—anything to redirect the pain. Some people can easily block out the images of hungry children begging in the streets. I used to do that too. But now that I was here, I couldn't. I wanted to run down to the streets, round them up, welcome them into my suite, and order every item on the room service menu. Instead, I closed my eyes and soaked my pillow with tears.

The following morning, my driver deposited me at Mark Buntain's office. Mark stood from behind the desk when I entered. He was a tall man with dark-rimmed glasses and thinning hair, his smile inviting, his handshake firm.

"Please, sit down," he said, pointing. "Just working on Sunday's sermon. Did you sleep well?"

"Not really," I confessed. "Lots of questions and emotions. I've never seen poverty like this. How do you and

Huldah keep from getting overwhelmed by all the need around you?"

"We stay focused on what we can do—not what we can't," he replied. "We were never asked to play God—that's his job. We can't do everything, but that can't be an excuse for doing nothing."

For two weeks, I shadowed Mark and Huldah with pen and notepad in hand. I thought I was there to write a book. But it was obvious God and the Buntains had another purpose in mind. This was a boot camp of sorts, and I was about to get my hands dirty and my heart for the poor resuscitated. Each day consisted of delivering food to widows, teaching orphans, caring for the elderly, or comforting patients in their hospital.

"To write our book," Mark explained, "you have to first understand the heart of our work." It took me a few days, but I finally understood his plan. Like a drill sergeant, he was trying to break me down and build me back up. I came to him as a writer; he wanted me to leave as a revolutionary.

This writing project was a far cry from my previous book. For that assignment, I had traveled to Miami's South Beach to interview eight multimillionaires and record their principles for success. Over six days, I rubbed shoulders with the rich and famous. I lost count of the Rolexes and Rolls-Royces, Birkins and Bentleys. I feasted on lobster and caviar and lounged in hot tubs. For a kid who grew up on food stamps and wore donated clothes, I felt like I'd won the lottery. But it didn't last. I returned home with a suitcase full of newfound discontent—until the invitation to fly to Kolkata came my way. It was there that my hopes, dreams, and fears changed with one disruptive conversation with Mother Teresa.

As the airplane taxied to the runway for my return to the States, I put my fatigued head against the window and stared at nothing. *I'm glad God called the Buntains and Mother Teresa to Kolkata and not me,* I thought. There was no denying I'd fallen in love with the Indian people and culture, but they also reminded me of everything I wasn't doing with my life. Every private conversation with the Buntains invalidated the life goals I'd adopted in South Beach. My entire life I had dreamed of escaping the poverty of my adolescence and making a name for myself. I grew up a nobody with holes in his shoes. I wanted to prove to everyone (including me) that I *was* somebody.

But now I found myself yearning for something more. It was difficult to describe, but I saw something in the Buntains and Mother Teresa that I needed. They had a deeper purpose and greater fulfillment than anyone I'd ever met. They didn't see kindness and compassion as sporadic, finite events, when you do something nice for someone and they feel better and so do you. No, they challenged me to see kindness as a lifestyle. "Otherwise," Huldah said, "you won't see other people's needs as opportunities to do something kind."

The airplane lifted off and I took one final glance at Kolkata. I could almost see Mother Teresa's words painted in large white letters on the tarmac: "Everyone can do something." I couldn't hold back the nagging questions any longer. I whispered, "Why am I here? What's my mission? What can I do?" I awaited God's answer—but all I heard was the hum of jet engines. Fortunately, it was an eight-hour flight—enough time for God and me to figure out what I was supposed to do with my life.

Discovering and defining your mission is like preparing for the obstacle course on *American Ninja Warrior.* You have to know your mission—and its demands—before you know how to prepare. You can't just crash the set and announce to the show's producers, "I'm here! Put me on." There are practical steps you must take to prepare yourself mentally and physically. Here are steps you can take to help you define your mission and prepare for the task ahead.

STEPS TO DEFINE YOUR MISSION

1. Create a Bucket List

If you're under thirty, you belong to what I call the "Bucket List Generation." Your parents and grandparents probably waited until they were fifty to prepare their list. You may have written yours when you were ten. Irrespective of where you fall, undoubtedly you have things you want to experience over the course of your life. With the internet, you have access to the most information in history. Regardless of your age, the world is yours to explore and to influence. Write down the places you want to visit, things you want to experience, and people you want to meet. And don't stop there. Write down what you want to give back to the world too. It's a fallacy to think your bucket list must be entirely self-serving. You can begin with experiences like skydiving or an Alaskan expedition and include feeding hungry children, protecting the environment, or helping veterans find employment. Once you have your list, keep it where you can see it. Add to it as you experience more of life and as your hopes and dreams evolve. And cross things off as you go. The list isn't meant to be a static piece of paper; it should be something you pray and dream about.

To give you some inspiration as you compose your list, here are a few items from my bucket list:

- Walk the red carpet at a Hollywood premiere.
- Watch a tennis match at Wimbledon.
- Visit Antarctica.
- Raise my children to be kind and generous.
- Inspire a network of revolutionaries who practice disruptive compassion.
- Feed one million children each day.
- Train and mobilize one million people for service every year.
- Write a personal manifesto.

Let me explain what I mean by manifesto. That is a statement that declares what you value and defines how you're going to live that out. It's a document you have to own—otherwise you'll never be sufficiently invested. Each person's manifesto is different. This is not a file you pull up on your computer every New Year's Eve. Your manifesto holds you accountable each day for your values, priorities, and activities. One team described a manifesto as a statement of principles and a bold, sometimes rebellious, call to action. The manifesto challenges assumptions, fosters commitment, and provokes change.[1]

The Declaration of Independence and Dr. Martin Luther King Jr.'s "I Have a Dream" speech are examples of manifestos. Some modern-day manifestos include the Holstee manifesto, the Expert Enough manifesto, the Focus manifesto, and the Steal Like an Artist manifesto.

While writing this book, I decided it was time to cross "manifesto" off my bucket list. Below you'll find what I came up with. It's a manifesto for anyone wanting to be a revolutionary who practices disruptive compassion.

The Disruptive Compassion Manifesto

- HOPE. Refuse to lose it.
- The world is hurting, but SOMETHING can ALWAYS be done.
- The status quo is overrated. Better *is* BETTER and possible *is* POSSIBLE.
- SACRIFICE is not a burden.
- Always do the NEXT KIND thing.
- LOVE simply—God, people, planet.
- TOMORROW doesn't excuse today; it DEPENDS on it.
- Be IMPATIENT (for justice) and intolerant (of hatred).
- Expect obstacles and KEEP GOING.
- BECOME a revolutionary.

2. Get Uncomfortable

If you're married to comfortable, then you've already set the ceiling for your impact. The pursuit of your mission will be limited to that sphere. It's a fact: some people are simply more adventurous than others. They have a higher distress tolerance and fewer inhibitions and anxieties. (I wish I had inherited that gene.) But those qualities don't make certain people better or more valuable; it just means they're more likely to fulfill their mission by living in a dung hut in Africa. Maybe you'll fulfill your mission on Wall Street or in a library or classroom. One path is not inherently more valuable than the other.

If you need to gauge your distress tolerance before setting off on a particular trail of disruptive compassion, you might find these questions helpful. But don't let them inhibit you from breaking out of your comfort zone.

- Do you need a Starbucks within driving distance?
- Do you want cell coverage 24/7?
- Do you need high-definition television?
- Do you need a car?
- Do you want a mattress?
- Do you mind spiders and mosquitos?
- Do you require Netflix?
- Do you need air-conditioning?
- Do you bathe in rivers and ponds?
- Do you want to learn another language?
- Do you eat large bugs?
- Do you jump out of airplanes?

Obviously these questions lean toward the extreme. Every mission doesn't require the same level of endurance or sacrifice. But an unwillingness to endure any level of discomfort is a limitation to your life of disruptive compassion. If that describes you, try stepping out of your comfort zone in a small way. Breaking free is not always geographical—sometimes it's experiential. Do something you haven't done before: introduce yourself to the person standing next to you in line; sign up for a cooking class; juggle or do magic tricks for kids at an elementary school; donate blood; start a "chain of generosity" at the next drive-thru you visit, paying for the person behind you; write someone an email or letter of encouragement. The opportunities are endless.

Comfort zones minimize our impact by conditioning us to settle for less than the best. Writer Matt Valentine notes, "At some point in life . . . we grow tired and settle for what we have. This is perhaps the worst fate of all. Because while you're technically still alive, you go on to live as if you were dead, settling into a life which doesn't truly make you happy and never taking any chances. Worse, at this point in your life, when you are posed with an opportunity, you'll begin to pull back (often unconsciously) for fear of losing access to your bubble of comfort."[2]

Martin Luther King Jr. addressed this topic too: "You may be thirty-eight years old, as I happen to be. And one day, some great opportunity stands before you and calls you to stand up for some great principle, some great issue, some great cause. And you refuse to do it because you are afraid. . . . Well, you may go on and live until you are ninety, but you're just as dead at thirty-eight as you would be at ninety. And the cessation of breathing in your life is but the belated announcement of an earlier death of the spirit."[3]

You won't earn a badge or patch to sew on a vest for stepping out of your comfort zone. Often it goes unnoticed because your comfort zone is invisible and the determination it requires is also hard to see. But progress *is* visible. The more you stretch yourself, the more change you will see. And as you change, those in your circle of influence may follow your lead and begin expanding their comfort zones. So don't be surprised if one day you see them "jumping out of airplanes" too.

3. Take a Road Trip

You may have scored 35 on your ACT or have a PhD behind your name, but you still have a lot to learn. You won't learn it glued to Instagram, Snapchat, Facebook, or whatever platform is the current craze. Some aspects of life have to be seen or experienced before you can fully appreciate them. So open your eyes and observe the myriad of needs around you: schools that need painting, nursing homes that deserve laughter, neighborhoods that need cleanup, public servants who deserve appreciation, schoolteachers who need assistance in their classroom, churches or civic organizations that need support, and more. You'll discover a world of opportunity in your own back yard.

Find a way to connect with the plight of suffering people—either in your community or in a developing country. Until you've witnessed suffering personally (not online or on television), your heart may be less compelled to respond. It doesn't feel real. Take the steps necessary to disrupt your life by placing yourself with others in need. You don't have to leave the continent, either. There are hurting and lonely people within a few miles of your home or college dorm.

Force yourself to face any hidden prejudices and question your assumptions. For example, as you drive, you'll likely encounter someone holding a sign that says "Hungry—will work for food." They're often described as panhandlers, con artists, and freeloaders. After all, you've probably heard the stories of sign holders making $80,000 a year and living in 3,000-square-foot homes. However, a survey of 146 sign holders in San Francisco revealed:

- 60 percent make $25 a day or less.
- 94 percent use the money for food.
- 82 percent are homeless.[4]

A study by the Denver Foundation showed that public perceptions of the causes of homelessness didn't line up with reality. Those surveyed believed the causes to be unemployment, substance abuse, and mental illness. In fact, the primary causes are the loss of a job, rising housing costs, and the breakup of a family. The Denver study also revealed that 64 percent of the homeless in the city are families with children; 42 percent are women; and one-third are actually working.[5]

Amid a growing epidemic of need, obviously you can't fix every problem or respond to every crisis. You can't rescue every sign holder or guarantee a warm bed to every homeless person. Just because you see a need doesn't obligate you to make it your mission. Should you practice disruptive compassion? Yes. Should you launch a crusade? Not necessarily. It's one thing to hand sign holders five dollars and say, "God bless you." It's quite another to dedicate your life to rescuing them from the streets. So how do you distinguish between one act of compassion and your life's calling? If you believe in God, ask him to show you what he wants done. The rest of the mental process often goes like this:

- You see a need that grabs your attention.
- You say, "Someone needs to do something about that."
- You begin asking, "Is there something I feel compelled to do?" (If not, this is not your mission.)
- You define (or write) your mission.
- You formulate a plan with desired outcomes.
- You recruit partners.
- You take action.

After visiting Kolkata, I was tempted to sell everything I owned, wave goodbye to my friends, and move to India. (I could live without Krispy Kremes if I had to.) But through reflection and prayer, I knew I was being driven by shame rather than by my calling. I felt guilty for having so much when others had so little. It wasn't fair. I did nothing to deserve my circumstances and they'd done nothing to deserve theirs. But that didn't justify moving halfway around the world. The Buntains were fulfilling *their* mission in life—and were worthy of all my support—but deep down I knew the search for my mission had to continue.

4. Demote Some "Friends"

If you're in a self-serving rut—and all you can think about is what movie to watch on Saturday or what takeout to pick up later—make an effort to spend time with people who will disrupt your status quo. (That's what the Buntains did for me—they changed my normal course.) You'll never discover your mission by hanging out with people whose goal in life is to have a good time and find their bliss. You may need to demote them from a leading role to the supporting cast. Instead, you need friends who, at one time or another, will say, "Get off your rear and do something productive and meaningful for the world. The excuse of 'tomorrow' expired yesterday. Your good intentions aren't matching up with your day-to-day decisions. If you want this year to be different, you have to do something differently."

Surrounding yourself with the right voices means making sure you don't encircle yourself with professional complainers. We all know people who think they can change the world by pointing fingers and casting blame. But frankly, they'd accomplish a lot more by shutting up and just loving someone. Don't you think it's time CIA wannabes scrap their surveillance missions and stop trying to change the world one gossip at a time?

The truth is there will always be complainers, gossipers, and slanderers, but it's up to you to decide how much time you spend with them. You choose whether to give their voices influence in your life. And those choices have critical consequences. If you spend your days with complainers and gossipers, before long you'll begin sounding like them. Seriously, have you ever considered doing everyone a favor and telling them the truth? Something like, "Listen, I love you and want the best for you, so let me give you some advice. It's up to you whether you hear it. But I think you need to take a break from all the complaining and gossiping. It's not healthy. Instead, try focusing more on the positives, and when you're frustrated, look for ways to show a little more patience, understanding, and kindness." Hopefully your friendship can survive the candor, but if it doesn't, perhaps it wasn't the most beneficial relationship anyway. They may unfriend you on Facebook and delete you from their phone, but someday they'll likely thank you for caring enough to tell them what they didn't want to hear.

The more you and your circle of friends share the same ethnicity or background, attend the same school, and belong to the same organization or socioeconomic group, the more challenging it will be to develop a diversified worldview. Without realizing it, you may belong to an unofficial affinity group—associating with people who share your perspective. And although there's nothing inherently wrong with that (to some extent we all do it), be aware that it may prevent you from growing in your understanding of other cultures and viewpoints. According to Professor Katherine W. Phillips of Columbia Business School, studies have shown that "being around people who are different from us makes us more creative, more diligent, and harder working."[6]

The internet can expose us to a diversity of people and opinions. With a click of a button or tap of a screen, we can connect with people around the globe. But with that access also come risks. Advances in technology, for example, may also be pushing us toward self-segregation. As Danah Boyd said, "The tools that were designed to bring people together are [being] used by people to magnify divisions and undermine social solidarity. . . . It's a fact: while Americans have countless tools with which to connect with one another, we are also watching fragmentation, polarization, and de-diversification happen en masse. The American public is self-segregating, tearing at the social fabric of the country."[7]

Finding and defining your mission may require you to be more purposeful in the formation of your friend group. That doesn't mean you should diversify your circle of friends just so you can check all the boxes. Sincerity and common sense can't be chucked out the window. But it does call for you to examine who's speaking into your life—and who's not. Are your best friends bringing different perspectives and experiences that will help you define and fulfill your mission? If not, perhaps it's time to make some changes. With the help of your friends, you can cut through the noise—all those priorities, interests, and invitations competing for your attention—and decide what mark you want to make on the world.

5. Do Something Great

Bucket lists and manifestos are meaningless unless they're followed by action. You have to fight the temptation to become paralyzed by the magnitude of the aspiration and the massive needs of the world. Cling to what Mother Teresa said: "Everyone can do something." One more "something" is better than nothing.

Remember, your mission isn't to sanitize the world. No—your job is to love people. Everyone can do that. It's one thing to build an image for being kind and generous. It's another level to earn a reputation for demonstrating love to people who just need to know someone cares. Saint Augustine said, "What does [love] look like? It has hands to help others, feet to hasten to the poor and needy, eyes to see misery and want, ears to hear the sighs and sorrows of men. That is what love looks like."[8]

Have you ever wondered why we talk so much about love—and say we care so much about the condition of the world—but do so little? For most, it's not that they lack compassion. It's because they lack confidence. They've raised their hands in surrender to fear, uncertainty, and doubt. People need to believe again that they can make a significant difference in the world.

In his mission to save the world, Jesus faced opposition and hardship. Everywhere he went, he encountered hungry, diseased, and lonely people. He didn't help everyone, but without prejudice, he was willing to stop and help anyone. As his disciple John said, "Let's not merely say that we love each other; let us show the truth by our actions" (1 John 3:18 NLT).

When my mother passed away, no one at her funeral talked about her house, her 401k, or her bank account. They didn't mention her job title or awards. They talked about her kindness, humility, mercy, and love. They focused on who she was and what she did for others. In her final days, she didn't look back on her life with regret. She had dedicated herself to service, and that's how she was remembered. How do you want to be remembered? In a sense, your manifesto is the first draft of the obituary that will one day be read in your honor.

WHERE DO I FIT?

You might be saying, "Yeah, there's hope for the world, but I don't see my place in it." Don't write yourself off. And while you're at it, bodyslam the guilt. No one expects you to carry the weight of the world on your shoulders. You may be overworked, overburdened, overwhelmed, and overtaxed. That's your reality. You can still practice disruptive compassion. Begin with your family and friends and invite them to take the journey with you. Don't let anyone tell you you're stuck. If you don't like your life, stop playing a victim. Be honest with yourself. You may be a willing participant. You can change your course. But when you do, make sure you're headed in the right direction. The wrong opportunity can lead to a miserable place. If you make mistakes, retrace your steps and get back on track. Just don't give up.

Set high goals. Dream big. Imagine the impossible. Don't be afraid to attempt something great and then fail. Failure is not failure—it's an education. Through your mistakes you'll learn what really helps people and what doesn't. You'll figure out what gets you farther down the road and what sets you back. But keep trying. Take that first step—no matter how large or small—and learn from it. Then take another step. That's how movements begin.

Essentially, that's how Convoy of Hope got its start. After returning from Kolkata, I felt compelled to do something. Along with some friends, I began loading pickup trucks and U-Haul trailers with food and distributing it to working-poor families in California. And that's how my mission found me.

You can begin to discover *your* mission by asking two simple questions:

1. "What needs do I see in the world?"
2. "What needs do I still need to see?"

Perhaps you've already found your mission—you saw a

need in your community and you're doing what you can to address it. But if you're still searching for your place and purpose, think of yourself as Indiana Jones embarking on a fact-finding mission. Through reconnaisance and research (discussed in chapter 3), you'll discover there's a mission out there waiting just for you.

DO RECONNAISSANCE

*A knight sets out to illuminate the darkness in
society, not from its leaves but from its roots. This
is how justice will be realized. Find the source.*

—Ethan Hawke

B ye, Mom and Dad," I said, waving from our driveway.
Dad smiled as he backed their vehicle past the family
bicycle.

Mom rolled down her window and hollered, "Help the
babysitter. We won't be gone long."

*I'm twelve; why do we even need a babysitter? I can handle my
younger brothers and five-year-old sister.*

Two hours later, police officers arrived at our door. They
came to deliver the news that my parents never made it to
the business meeting. They were hit head-on by a drunken
driver. My dad was killed instantly and my mom was still
fighting for her life.

Friends and neighbors gathered in our front yard and the
police officers stepped to the porch to address the crowd.

"Are there any family members or friends who will take the four children home with them tonight? If not, we'll take them downtown to the station."

That night, Bill and Louvada Davis invited us to stay with their family in their single-wide trailer. At the time, they probably thought it would be a short sleepover. Instead, we lived with them for many months while Mom recovered from broken bones and internal injuries. The Davises sacrificed their privacy and drained their savings account so four kids could have a home. They modeled disruptive compassion.

In time, we moved to a place of our own. But that was the beginning of some difficult years. My parents didn't have insurance, nor did the man who hit them. And to make matters worse, Mom's recovery lasted many months, which delayed her return to the workforce. As a result, our family was forced to survive on welfare and food stamps.

I resented what my life had become.

I wasn't picking fights, throwing temper tantrums, or disobeying teacher instructions. I was just struggling to make sense of it all. *It's my job to be strong for my brothers and sisters,* I preached to myself. *Dad and Mom would want me to keep the family together.* I tried to bury my questions, but I could always feel them bubbling to the surface. Then one day when I was alone, the volcano erupted and my hot tears flowed like lava.

"God, you say you're so powerful, but why didn't you protect Mom and Dad?" I demanded. "What did they ever do to deserve this? Why didn't you stop this from happening? You left us with nothing. Dad is dead and I hear my mom crying night after night. Tell me how that's fair."

To me, that felt like an ideal time for an angel to appear with a message from God. The angel could tell me, "You know, everything is going to be okay. God is with you. Your dad is in heaven and he's doing well. Don't worry, your mom is going to make it through the surgeries just fine. And, oh, I've arranged for you to win the lottery so you won't have any money worries." Then maybe I'd feel better. Then maybe I'd believe it was going to be okay.

Instead, complete silence.

"God," I blurted, "either you don't exist, you have no power, you don't care, or you're evil."

I was hoping that would at least get his attention. Any sign he was listening would do: flickering lights, a creaking door, or "Hi, I'm your angel, Gabe."

Still nothing. Obviously accusations weren't working, so I attempted a different approach. "God," I said, "I believe you exist and have a crazy amount of power—look at the planets and stars you created. Saturn is, like, so cool. And I really do think you care and I know you're not evil. That only leaves one option: you let this happen for a reason. Frankly, I'm *not* okay with that. He was my dad. I don't care what reason you have, you abandoned me. You say you're all about love and justice. Right now I'm not so sure. How can the man who killed my father be out of jail partying while we're sentenced to a life of poverty? God, where are you? Do you even hear me?"

The Bible is filled with the stories of people who pointed their fingers at God and lived to tell about it. I figured God wasn't easily offended by harsh questions and emotional outbursts. Maybe I was fooling myself, but I assumed he appreciated the honesty. I wasn't worried that he'd serve me bad sushi or flatten my tires because I called him out. I just wanted him to know that I felt like he stood me up that day and I wasn't happy about it. He could have sent a sign that he was with me, but he chose not to. He could have done something to dry my tears, but he didn't. He could have saved my dad and stopped that driver, but he didn't. Sure, it felt good to speak my mind—and venting probably saved me plenty on counseling bills—but my questions lingered like a bad case of bronchitis.

My unending attempt to answer unanswerable questions ultimately led to fear, frustration, anxiety, anger, inferiority, and discouragement. Though only a teenager, I was suffering from analysis paralysis. I knew I had a choice: I could allow my questions to steal my chances at happiness, or I could come to terms with the fact that some questions will never be answered.

About the time I entered college, I made a decision that helped me find peace and freedom. There was a lot I didn't understand about God's ways, and I wasn't ready to let him off the hook. But I refused to allow the drunk driver to destroy another life. I decided my future was in my hands, not his. I couldn't erase what he did to my family, but I had the power to put an end to the damage he was inflicting. I didn't have to play the role of a victim, bound by bitterness. Instead I could become my father's second wind and live a full life. With that new perspective, my anger at God subsided and I was no longer haunted by unanswerable questions. In time, painful memories began to fade too, and what I remembered most was the love and kindness shown to us by friends like the Davises.

After graduating from college, I stopped by Bill and Louvada's home one day. (They were no longer living in the single-wide trailer.) Their hair showed flecks of gray, but their smiles were just as soothing. That day I asked Louvada a question that had nipped at me for years. "After the accident, what compelled you to take four children into your home? I mean, your kids—Terri and Steve—gave up their bedrooms and shared their parents with us. That couldn't have been easy."

Without hesitation, she said, "We love your family. We knew it's what God wanted us to do. So we just did it—no questions asked." She removed her glasses and wiped her eyes.

"I know you gave up your privacy and spent money you didn't have," I said.

"We'd do it again," Bill said, fighting tears.

Years later, I would learn that Bill worked overtime at the rock quarry to feed his small army. There was so much I wanted to say to them and their children. But the lines in my head sounded like they'd been stolen from the Hallmark Channel. How do you tell someone you owe them your life? Their kindness had helped me overcome anger and bitterness—enemies that would have stolen my future. But at the moment, eloquent words were escaping me.

"Thanks for everything," I said, regretting I couldn't express the depth of my gratitude.

But words weren't needed. Bill promptly wrapped his arms around me and held me tight. Louvada followed with a hug of her own. Together we had endured tragedy and hardship and we were still standing. It was then that I realized the tragedy of my past hadn't dictated my future. I was exactly where I needed to be.

IDENTIFYING ENEMIES

We all have personal enemies that threaten to imprison us. They include fear, loneliness, resentment, regret, abuse, addiction, inferiority, jealousy, ambition, poverty, racism, and more. They endanger our happiness and often shift our focus from the world's needs to our own. When we're pre-occupied with our problems, it's more difficult to practice disruptive compassion. Generosity, for example, is a challenge when you can't pay your bills. Kindness is tough when you've been slandered. Stopping to help a stranger is difficult when you're battling fear. So how can you conquer your personal enemies so they don't interfere with your mission?

Corrie ten Boom, who endured injustice in a Nazi prison concentration camp, said, "The first step on the way to victory is to recognize the enemy." Revolutionaries do the same. They know their foes, which typically fall into one of three categories: personal, social, and spiritual. Personal enemies include circumstances, individuals, emotions, and experiences. Social enemies may be war, poverty, malnutrition, disease, and pollution. And if you're a person of faith, you believe in the existence of a spiritual enemy and forces of darkness.

The enemies of my childhood arrived at my door like three thugs attempting to kidnap my soul. They came in the form of anger, poverty, and inferiority. Every month a social worker came to our home to ensure we were still deserving of government assistance. I despised those interrogations. *Why should a child have to justify a new toy given by his grandmother?*

I also despised walking into school with holes in both my shoes and jeans (before holes were cool). Every lunch period reminded me I was different. I was eating mayonnaise sandwiches and off-brand peanut butter crackers. Meanwhile, my friends ate tuna fish, apples, and Hostess cupcakes. Needless to say, they'd never trade for anything I had to offer. We couldn't always afford a barber, so I grew my hair long and trimmed it myself. I detested standing in line at the grocery store with food stamps and confessing to my Little League coach I couldn't afford a new baseball glove.

But nothing was worse than being targeted by bullies. When you're labeled a poor kid, you get shoved in hallways, harrassed in the locker room, ignored by girls, and ridiculed when you're not looking. They laugh at your clothes and pretend you smell like dog manure. It's no wonder I suffered from class anxiety. I vowed that someday I wouldn't be poor, but most of the time I didn't have enough self-confidence to try. Those years helped me understand how poor families remain powerless for generations—they begin believing that they're third-class citizens. They suffer from what sociologists call social immobility.[1] They feel trapped in a pit of circumstances and don't know how to climb their way to freedom.

Some days, when I stepped onto my junior high campus, I felt like I was entering a prison yard. I could almost feel imaginary guards in towers following my every movement with binoculars. Here was my problem: I was letting other people define me. Just because I was poor didn't mean I was stupid. And just because I didn't have hundred-dollar basketball shoes didn't mean I couldn't dunk like Michael Jordan. (Well, I guess I couldn't—but occasionally I knocked down threes like Steph Curry.)

Your enemies want to define you. They want to limit your potential for good by telling you what you're not. Fortunately your enemies' opinions don't matter unless you believe them. Your job title doesn't define you. What car you drive, what neighborhood you live in, or what brand of clothes you wear doesn't define you either. You're defined by your character, kindness, generosity, and commitment. Your past (even a tragic auto accident) doesn't define you. It's simply the trail you've traveled thus far to get to where you want to go.

The more you're able to overcome personal enemies, the more effective you will be at combating social enemies like poverty, loneliness, disease, pollution, racism, war, and more. It's easy to look at the state of the world and assume we're losing. After all, sixteen thousand children die each day from hunger and water-related causes. The polar ice caps are melting. Teen suicide rates continue to climb. Terrorist attacks and school shootings are on the increase. But there is reason for optimism. Whether you believe in God or simply trust the human spirit, there is a lot of love in this world that can flow through you to defeat any enemy and solve every problem. Seriously, if you wake up most days with hope and optimism, there's no limit to the good you can accomplish. But without hope there can be no victory over the status quo. The Bible says, "Be prepared. You're up against far more than you can handle on your own. Take all the help you can get, every weapon God has issued, so that when it's all over but the shouting you'll still be on your feet" (Eph. 6:13 MSG).

PREPARING AND RESEARCHING

Preparation leads to greater accomplishment. Athletes practice to improve their games. Students crack the books to earn degrees. Stockbrokers study the marketplace to get ahead. A huge part of preparation is knowing what you're up against. That's where reconnaissance ("recon," or strategic research) comes in. It helps you learn the obstacles and tendencies of your enemies. Without recon, it's easy to magnify the size of your enemy and assume defeat is inevitable. You begin to focus on the obstacles rather than problem solving. But that fear is often based on false perceptions, and those false beliefs are based on propaganda.

Chinese general Sun Tzu said, "If you know the enemy and know yourself, you need not fear the result of a hundred battles. If you know yourself but not the enemy, for every victory gained you will also suffer a defeat. If you know neither the enemy nor yourself, you will succumb in every battle."[2]

Recon also builds confidence and understanding. The dictionary defines *reconnaissance* as "a preliminary survey to gain information—an exploratory military survey of enemy territory."[3] Recon specialists are neither assassins nor saboteurs. They don't sneak into enemy territory and set off explosions and knock off bad guys. Their duty—and your responsibility—is to gather information and return to camp undetected by the enemy. But here's what happens to you when you embark on a reconnaissance mission: you discover what you *can* do and what the enemy *can't*. You begin to see a path to success. Your confidence grows, and you find the courage to move forward with your mission.

Once you've identified an enemy, do some research and development. If, for example, you want to fight the enemy called hunger, proper reconnaissance will take you to its root causes. Find out what is being done to combat malnutrition—what's working and what's not. Study intervention opportunities and explore what assets you can leverage to be a part of the solution. (See chapter 4.)

Recon work may also require you to be intentional in exposing yourself to the world's suffering. This doesn't mean you have to take a vow of poverty or put yourself at risk. But it may mean serving soup in a food line, volunteering at a shelter, or skipping a few meals. On the other hand, if you want to confront the enemy of loneliness and depression, reach out to people who need a friend and learn more about their struggle. Whatever enemy you face, look for ways to gain greater knowledge and understanding before you take it on.

I grew up rooting for the San Francisco 49ers, so on a brisk December afternoon, when the Niners and Convoy of Hope came together to serve 1,200 impoverished families at Levi's Stadium in Santa Clara, California, it was a dream come true. Team chaplain Earl Smith, the champion of the event, enlisted Niners players and employees to provide hot meals, groceries, haircuts, shoes, Christmas gifts, and more. The players even took the kids out onto the field for football drills. Josh Richardson, cofounder of Angel Armor and a long-time supporter of Convoy of Hope, volunteered to work at the event. Josh and his family have donated generously to charities that help the hungry, hurting, and suffering. Giving is part of the family's DNA and the businesses they own. That evening, as Josh was distributing groceries off the back of a Convoy of Hope tractor trailer, he discovered the power of recon.

"When we started handing out groceries, it shook me in ways I never imagined," he said. "When we handed families the groceries, their faces lit up. It felt good to do something beyond writing a check. I got my hands dirty. It opened my eyes to the fight against poverty and hopelessness. It transformed me. When my knuckles brushed against theirs, I realized how insulated I'd been. For the first time, I could feel their pain."

Academy Award–winning actor Adrien Brody had a profound experience of his own after playing the lead role in

The Pianist. To prepare himself for his role as Polish-Jewish composer and Holocaust survivor Wladyslaw Szpilman, he gave up his car, apartment, and telephones. He moved to Europe with two suitcases and went on a crash diet to lose thirty pounds. "There is an emptiness that comes with really starving that I hadn't experienced," he said. But for a year after making the film, Brody said he suffered from depression and mourning. "I was very disturbed by what I embraced [in making that film]," he said, "and of the awareness that it opened up in me."[4]

Recon will prepare you for your mission, and as Josh and Adrien discovered, it might even change you. Once you've "brushed knuckles," it's more difficult to emotionally detach yourself from the needs around you. You begin to see people through a lens of compassion rather than one of condemnation. At one time you may have considered yourself superior to them. Not anymore. You're just grateful for the opportunities you have and feel compelled to help others experience a better life too.

As the Austrian Airlines jet prepared its descent into Sarajevo, Bosnia, I peered out the window in disbelief. It looked like a series of tornadoes had ravaged the city. The war between the Serbs, Croats, and Muslims had left buildings in ruin.

"Mortar shells," my driver later explained. "This has all been done by bullets, grenades, and mortar shells. Be careful where you walk. We still have thousands of landmines."

Every street corner laid claim to its own tragedy. "Here," the guide said, "ninety people were killed. Right over there, children were executed."

The streets were dark, the buildings gutted. It was hard to comprehend the city was once teeming with pedestrians.

When we passed a city park, my photographer ordered, "Please stop right here—we want to see this." If the destruction of infrastructure wasn't enough to shake me, this was. The park had been converted to a graveyard. Swing sets and slides were surrounded by mounds of dirt and makeshift gravestones. *How can anyone claim victory in a war like this?* I asked myself. *The memories will scar the children here for a lifetime.*

The photographer walked across the park, leaving me alone to stare at the gravesites. Nearby I noticed an elderly woman wiping tears from her eyes and a man with his dog. It was obvious this park no longer belonged to children.

As we drove away, I asked the driver, "How did the war end?"

"The sides got tired of fighting—they finally talked to one another."

"I guess the more you get to know someone, the harder it is to hate them," I said.

The driver nodded. "They should have talked *before* they started shooting."

Sometimes recon reveals that the greatest obstacle to ending crises and defeating such enemies as poverty and pollution is our anemic will. As revolutionaries, we have to *want* change before we'll ever *see* change.

GAINING PERSPECTIVE

Military battles are often waged on multiple fronts (air, land, and sea). At times, I've felt surrounded by *my* enemies, as if they were attacking from different flanks. Perhaps you know that feeling. It's like a barrage of problems all at once: broken relationships, financial setbacks, physical challenges, career disappointments. You're tempted to enter witness protection just to preserve your sanity. But during those trying times, I've gained perspective and peace by praying, reading Scripture, and talking to friends. How does that work? The Bible says when you come close to God, he will come close to you. (See James 4:8.) For me, that's the highest form of recon and the most reliable intel I can get.

One evening I tried to share that insight with a fellow passenger on a flight to Florida. For the first thirty minutes, we talked about our respective vocations, hometowns, hobbies, and families. The usual.

Without warning, he began wiping tears from his face.

"You okay?" I asked.

"Been going through a rough stretch," he replied. "My daughter tried to take her life."

"I'm really sorry," I said. "I'll definitely remember you and your family in my prayers."

"Thanks, but I'm really not into that stuff anymore. I don't believe it does any good. Right now I need a lot more than a crutch."

"For what it's worth, I agree with you," I said. "Prayer *is* a crutch. But I don't think there's anything wrong with that. If the God who created the universe is listening, hey, I can use all the help I can get. If no one is listening, at least it makes me feel better."

With a furrowed brow, he said, "I lost my faith a long time ago. And I'm not sure what I believe now. But what you just said actually makes sense."

"Give it a try," I said. "I believe he's listening and wants to help. This is the third flight I was scheduled to be on today. The other two were canceled. Maybe he arranged this whole thing because he wanted you to know he cares."

"You're not one of those angels, are you?" he said with a grin.

"No, sir—not even close."

Reconnaissance helps you find your mission by identifying your enemies, preparing and researching, and gaining perspective. The next step is to determine what assets you have to accomplish your mission. Because when you conduct an audit, you'll likely discover you have more at your disposal than you think.

CHAPTER 4

CONDUCT AN AUDIT

Life is very interesting . . . in the end, some of
your greatest pains become your greatest strengths.

—Drew Barrymore

I'm not Bill Gates—what difference can I really make here?"
That was the burning question as I trudged through Mathare Valley, a slum in Nairobi, Kenya, inhabited by 700,000 people. No running water. No electricity. No sewage system. It looked like a city of children's forts—tiny hovels made of tin, plastic, and plywood. *Where do we even start?*

Our guide—a young man who lived in Mathare—hollered, "Follow me." As we descended farther into the slum past some stern-faced men, I started to wonder if this was safe. A gunshot rang out in the distance. I guess that was my answer.

"That is far away," he reassured. "Come!" My photographer and I exchanged worried glances.

"What do you want us to see?" I asked.

He pointed. "This."

There, on a patch of dirt, eleven boys lay motionless.

"What's this?" I asked. "Are they sleeping?"

The guide shook his head. "No, they sniff glue to take away their hunger. Some even use drops of jet fuel to get high."

I had no response.

Nearby, I watched dozens of children scavenge for food on a mountain of garbage. These kids were living in an abyss with no way out.

I didn't smile for three days. How could I? What if they were *my* kids? Could I just "get over it" then?

My colleague sensed I was struggling. "You never get used to seeing hungry kids," he said.

"It isn't fair—these kids didn't choose to be born into this life," I said. "I wish there was something we could do."

"I know Convoy of Hope is just getting started," he said, "but someday you could help a lot of people in Africa."

"It would take a lot more money and workers than we have," I said.

"I think you have greater potential and more resources than you realize," he countered.

That sounded promising, but seriously, what did we have that could transform Mathare Valley? I was in my thirties, paying down a mortgage, driving a refurbished car, and trying to keep food on the table for a wife and two kids. What could I realistically offer Mathare?

Despite my doubts, I posed the question: "What do we have, and what can we do?" That question was the first step toward Convoy of Hope establishing a feeding program for one thousand children at a school in Mathare Valley. It all began with an internal audit and the discovery of new resources and opportunities.

The world has enough resources to address the greatest problems of our time—hunger, pollution, poverty, and more. Still, millions suffer and our world deteriorates, largely because we don't fully know our potential. It's easier to blame our inaction on a lack of resources than to acknowledge what we have at our disposal. It's the "I can't do everything so I do nothing" excuse. Maybe you don't have as much power as you wish you had, but you definitely have more assets than you realize. As a revolutionary, you endeavor to maximize your assets and strive for greater outcomes. Golfing legend Arnold Palmer said, "The secret of concentration is the secret of self-discovery. You reach inside yourself to discover your personal resources and what it takes to match them to the challenge."

Have you ever told yourself, "I don't have enough clothes"? Then you clean out your closet and discover shirts and sweaters long forgotten? Internal auditing is much like that. It's a "verification activity." It tells you what assets you have and identifies waste and weaknesses in your systems. Hopefully, about now you're connecting the dots. You're saying to yourself, "I need to conduct my own internal audit. Maybe I'm not as limited on resources as I thought." Good—you got it. Next, let's break down five assets that can contribute to disruptive compassion: passion, voice, finances, network, and time.

PASSION

"When we talk about having a life of significance and meaning, it's not about fame or money or resources," said athlete Tim Tebow. "It's about people and lives and hearts. That's my biggest passion in life." In other words, life is not about how much we possess—it's about how much we can give away.

For Tebow, his faith plays a major role in establishing his priorities. Faith and passion have been at the foundation of some of the greatest protest movements in US history. From the American Revolution to the emancipation of slaves to the civil rights movement, faith has propelled activists to risk their lives and resources for a cause. George Washington, Abigail Adams, Rosa Parks, and many other revolutionaries believed they were on a mission greater than themselves. It was their duty and passion to make the world a better place.

Consider what social issues monopolize your thoughts and conversations. That's probably what we call passion—and passion is power. Every revolutionary has it. Passion drives you to greater achievement. If you're concerned about equal rights, for example, passion will motivate you to speak up and direct your assets to your cause. "The place where your treasure is, is the place you will most want to be, and end up being" (Matt. 6:21 MSG).

At times, passion and fervor can also drive people to do the wrong thing. Like a young man I heard about who boarded a plane for Chile to respond to an earthquake. He packed his suitcases with food and a backpack with bottled water. He had good intentions, but he didn't have experience in disaster relief. Nor did he do his homework. He didn't know that most disaster zones are off limits for uncertified personnel, and some governments have restrictions on what food can be brought into the country. When he arrived, he was forced to make like a tourist and spend a week in a hotel. More good could have been accomplished had he simply sent a donation to a reputable charity or church or offered his services to a relief organization. Instead, he wasted time and money trying to be a self-appointed first responder. Misdirected passion is typically ineffective. Focused passion, paired with education and preparation, is a force to be reckoned with.

VOICE

On her sixteenth birthday, Disney actress Zendaya announced to her family and friends that she didn't want a party or presents. Instead, she asked them and her social media followers to contribute to her cause. She wanted to empower women in Africa through Convoy of Hope's jobs training program. Subsequently, the campaign raised thousands in contributions. Since then, the star of *Spider-Man* and *The Greatest Showman* has continued to use her voice on her birthday to raise funds for special causes, including feedONE and Hurricane Harvey relief. Anyone—famous or not—can use their unique voice to help those whose voices can't be heard.

To this day I've never laughed so hard. I can't explain why the video was so contagious, but it was. And I had to share the video with my family and friends. As it turned out, I wasn't the only one. The next day, Candace Payne discovered her Facebook Live video had reached 24 million views overnight.

Before the world knew her name, Candace was a stay-at-home mom. Even then, while trying to make ends meet, she sought ways to be an "extravagant giver." She gave her church a few dollars extra each month, sold crocheted caps and gave the money to people in need, and even gave a stranger her last twenty dollars at a fast food restaurant.

One day, she returned some leggings to a department store and used the credit, a coupon, and some birthday money to purchase a Star Wars Chewbacca mask. She donned the mask in her minivan and went live on Facebook. That moment of "extravagant laughter" would change her life.

"I had a million views before I went to bed that night and it just took off," she said. To date, the video has been viewed 200 million times on Facebook alone. Candace has been featured on more than three thousand media outlets, including *Good Morning America* and *Cosmopolitan* magazine. More than 800,000 people befriended her on Facebook.

A few weeks after the video went viral, Candace recorded Michael Jackson's song "Heal the World," put it on iTunes, and gave the proceeds to Convoy of Hope. Since then, she has written two books and a joy-themed study guide and curriculum, and used her voice to inspire and motivate hundreds of thousands of people around the world. Her message is simple: "Laugh it up! Embrace freedom and experience defiant joy." Candace began using her voice for good long before she became a Facebook sensation.

Another example. Acapella singer-producer Mike Tompkins traveled to Tanzania to use his voice to help Convoy of Hope combat child hunger. He and his wife, Kayla, produced an original song and video that benefited the organization. It was the first time Mike had used his talents to raise awareness and funds for a charity. He usually makes videos for his YouTube channel and for companies like Pepsi and Microsoft. When the video launched, Mike challenged millions of his YouTube followers to speak up and join the effort to feed children around the world.

Or there's Vance McDonald, tight end for the Pittsburgh Steelers, who mobilized NFL players to help the poor and suffering. Besides helping to coordinate community outreaches, Vance and his wife, Kendi, traveled with Convoy of Hope and teammates to work at an orphanage in Haiti. And when Hurricane Harvey ravaged Houston, Vance and Kendi issued a matching challenge to other players and raised over

$100,000 for disaster relief. They have used their voices in the NFL to serve the poor and suffering.

And then there's Tampa Bay Buccaneers punter Bradley Pinion, who was named a finalist for NFL Man of the Year. Bradley took the opportunity to praise the disaster relief efforts of Convoy of Hope on national television. "They are one of the best at helping people when disasters strike," he said on the NFL Network. Earlier in the season, Pinion raised funds for the organization by painting our logo on his cleats and inviting his social media followers to join him in making a donation.

Celebrities often use the media to amplify their voices. Most of us don't have that kind of platform, but you don't have to be on YouTube or an NFL roster to make your voice count. Don't let anyone silence you. Speak up for what you believe and let people know what you stand for. Every movement begins with one voice that is amplified when joined by the voices of others.

Harvard Business Review studied how protests become successful social movements and reached this conclusion: "Throughout history, social movements—small groups that are loosely connected but united by a shared purpose—have created transformational change. Women's suffrage and civil rights in the US . . . hinged on the powerless banding together against the powerful. In these movements, protest has played an important role, highlighting the ability for ordinary citizens to make their disapproval heard. This type of activism is crucial for creating the groundwork for change."[1]

FINANCES

Curt and Nancy Richardson own OtterBox, a company that produces protective cases for mobile phones and tablets, among other things. They're innovators—they love taking risks and finding solutions to everyday problems. But simply accumulating more wealth isn't their primary goal. Curt, Nancy, and their two sons are passionate about helping people and giving to good causes. They also live with an unusual sense of gratitude.

"I married a serial entrepreneur and we survived some lean years early in our marriage," Nancy said, recalling the fledgling business that was started in their garage. "Sometimes friends and even strangers left groceries for us so we'd have food to eat. We learned quickly that money comes and goes, but giving and being grateful never has to."

OtterBox, headquartered in Fort Collins, Colorado, is based on the same principles that have guided the Richardsons from the beginning. The mission of OtterBox is "We grow to give."

In the summer of 2017, the Richardsons and OtterBox helped Convoy of Hope deliver millions of dollars' worth of emergency food, water, and supplies to the British Virgin Islands after they were decimated by two hurricanes. Days after the first hurricane, Curt went to the front lines of the disaster and worked alongside our teams for weeks on end. Under a sweltering sun and in thick humidity, Curt removed debris and distributed food and water. Meanwhile, back in Colorado, Nancy led a war room of employees and volunteers who jumped in to help with logistics, shipments of supplies, and fundraising for Convoy of Hope. "God has given us so much," she said. "We're just grateful we've been entrusted to help others—it's the most fulfilling thing we do."

Companies and movements succeed, in part, because they use their resources wisely. Companies like OtterBox, Hobby Lobby, DMP, and many others donate large portions of their profits to worthy causes. But financial health is a key factor in their longevity and impact. In much the same way, financial stability affects many areas of *your* life. Provided no one has shown up at your door holding helium balloons and an oversized check for $10 million, you probably have limited discretionary income. And, let's face it, if you're flat broke, you won't be heading to the movies, sporting events, or fancy dinners. Without money, your Amazon account is useless, your utilities will be turned off, and your ability to practice disruptive compassion is unavoidably affected. If you're up to your ears in credit card debt, you may hesitate to give twenty dollars to someone in need. That doesn't mean you have to own a car or real estate before you give. It just means poor financial health may limit what you can afford to give.

If you're serious about your pursuit of disruptive compassion, you need to be responsible for your financial health. If you don't like where you are today, take steps to get to a better place. Here are some basic questions to ask yourself:

1. What financial assets do I have?
2. Is there anything I can do to earn extra resources?
3. What are my expenses?
4. What is my current debt?
5. Where do I spend the most money?
6. Can I modify my spending habits?
7. Am I saving on a regular basis? Could I save more?
8. What is the maximum I can give away right now?
9. How much do I hope to be able to give away?

Although money is not the most important asset to a mission, no one can deny the role it can play in changing the world. Actor Michael J. Fox, who suffers from Parkinson's disease, said, "Medical science has proven time and again that when the resources are provided, great progress in the treatment, cure, and prevention of disease can occur."[2]

Some problems cannot be solved without resources. But you may be able to expand your donations through a matching gift program. For major social issues such as hunger, cancer, heart disease, and more, many corporations (and the government) offer matching gifts for their employees. An estimated $6 to $10 billion in matching gift funding goes *unclaimed* per year.[3] That's an insane amount of money to just be left on the table. Nearly two-thirds of large companies and 28 percent of small to midsize businesses offer to match employee donations.[4] Some companies are choosing to be certified as "B corporations." They strongly advocate community involvement and matching charitable donations among their employees. Whether a large corporation like Patagonia or Ben and Jerry's, or a small LLC, these companies are saying, "We care about more than just making money, and we want to hold ourselves to a higher standard." They exist for more than providing a product or service or making a profit—they want to make the world a better place through "conscientious capitalism."[5]

The challenge facing humanity is not just a scarcity of resources. It's the gathering, allocation, and delivery of those resources. Ignoring the doubters, one ten-year-old boy decided to take the matter into his own hands. Carson looks like any other standard-issue kid. Short hair, average size, but with eyes determined to change the world. Since he was five years old he's been dreaming of a way to help others. He found what he was searching for when he began raising money for Speed the Light and BGMC, organizations that purchase vehicles and equipment for missionaries and non-profits like Convoy of Hope.

"I saw a Convoy of Hope tractor trailer being unloaded," he said. "They were giving supplies to help people who had just made it through a disaster. I thought, *Man, it'd be cool to raise enough to give them another truck and trailer.*"

Carson set a goal of $150,000. To raise funds, he climbed up scaffolding and stayed on a ten-by-twenty-foot platform for several days with his father, Shawn, in a campaign dubbed the "Up in the Air Challenge." The duo slept on the platform, endured heavy winds, and even let people donate to shoot paintballs at them.

"I'll just keep on raising money because it's helping people," he said. "If I can do it, anyone can do it!"

Your finances—and the ability to generate resources—are a valuable asset that can make a world of difference.

NETWORK

Mother Teresa said, "I alone cannot change the world, but I can cast a stone across the waters to create many ripples." Robert F. Kennedy echoed that theme when he said, "Few will have the greatness to bend history itself, but each of us can work to change a small portion of events. It is from numberless, diverse acts of courage and belief that human history is shaped. Each time a man stands up for an ideal, or acts to improve the lot of others, or strikes out against injustice, he sends forth a tiny ripple of hope, and crossing each other from a million different centers of energy and daring those ripples build a current which can sweep down the mightiest walls of oppression and resistance."[6]

Take a moment to consider your network of friends.

Within that group is a collection of resources, ideas, and information (a Wikipedia of sorts) that has enormous potential for good. Convoy of Hope is an example of what can be accomplished when people with diverse skills and backgrounds come together. Each member of the team has embraced disruptive compassion and jumped the fences of their comfort zones to become revolutionaries in their own right.

Kimarie Page is a great example of one who rallied her friends to a worthy cause. When she heard about a trip to Africa hosted by Convoy of Hope, she said, "I don't even like to camp, let alone take a trip to Africa. And besides, we don't have the money." But a strong voice inside her was saying something was different about this trip. *I don't know why, but I know I'm supposed to go. I just know it,* she thought. Her husband agreed and they made it happen. On the trip, she was so profoundly moved by the sight of hungry children being fed that she vowed to do her part to feed even more. She returned to the States and began collecting spare change from her friends and students at schools in her area. In the end, she lugged more than one ton of coins to the bank equaling $45,000. Yes—$45,000. And that was just the beginning of her partnership with Convoy of Hope.

Ask yourself, are there churches, charities, schools, or civic organizations that you can network with now to expand your circle of relationships? Are there groups you can align with that share your passion? If so, that's an untapped resource that could increase your impact immediately.

TIME

It was the phone call my daughter, Lindsay, never expected, especially at Christmas during her senior year in high school.

She learned her best friend had died. Later that night, tears gave way to shock as she shoved food around her plate without eating. "It's like I'm out to sea—I'm numb," she confessed. "She was my go-to person, and now she's gone."

As her father, I felt helpless and uncertain too. Nothing I could say would take away the pain. My wife, Doree, and I just held Lindsay in our arms until she drifted asleep. If you're a parent, you know how tough it is to see your children suffer. There are no bandages for a broken heart.

The following morning, another friend of Lindsay's arrived at the door with a bag of snacks and a stack of DVDs. She gave Lindsay a long, sincere hug as if holding her together. Then, for two days, they sat together on the couch watching episodes of *Grey's Anatomy*. Sure, there were occasional tears, but the two seldom conversed. The friend knew—no matter what she did—she couldn't speed up the healing process. But she was there. She showed up. She stayed. This wasn't a counseling session. It was a friend offering what she could—her time.

Internal audits evaluate how you spend your time, which is your most valuable commodity. Let me stop right here and acknowlege that discussions on time management usually lead to depressing, judgmental thoughts: *How dare you watch television when you could be solving the world's pollution crisis?* Or, *If you spent more time fixing things around the house and less time playing golf, you'd have more money to take your dream vacation and more to give to your church or charity.* (Don't worry, I don't intend to add to your guilt.)

Each person controls his or her own alarm clock. You can push the snooze button as many times as you want. It's your life. You don't need to feel guilty for watching television or for swinging a golf club, as long as personal gratification hasn't become your highest priority. As actress Ellie Kemper of *The Office* and *Unbreakable Kimmy Schmidt* joked, "A man's face is not a rich person's lawn; you are wasting resources if you devote that much energy to trimming your beard, sideburns, or mustache just so."[7]

How you spend your time is the fingerprint—the identifier—of your priorities. Just as your prints tell the world who you are, how your time is spent tells the world what you value. So you may have to modify your calendar of activities if you want to leave a profound mark on the world. No, you don't have to give up your favorite hobby (life should be fun!), but you shouldn't view your time as a commodity to be spent carelessly either. You'll find more discretionary time when, with certain friends, you choose quality over quantity. Fewer conversations will make them more meaningful and less monopolizing. Bottom line: you have a limited supply of time, so use it with intentionality.

MULTIPLYING WHAT YOU HAVE

Jonathan McGuire, pastor at Bridge of Faith in Rockaway Beach, Missouri, wanted to do something to help his economically depressed community. He could have simply left Rockaway for another pastorate, but McGuire saw assets and potential others didn't see. Rather than accept the status quo and give up on the community, he decided to invest in its future. The church purchased an abandoned resort, with plans to refurbish the cabins and convert them into for-profit businesses that would stimulate the local economy and provide much-needed jobs. Those businesses include a coffee company, thrift store, and more. In turn, Bridge of Faith pours the profits back into the community to feed hundreds each week with the support of Convoy of Hope's Rural Compassion. McGuire is an example of entrepreneurs who have chosen to multiply their assets and expand their influence through innovation and determination.

Once your audit is complete and you know what resources you have, here's the next question to ask yourself: "What can I do to multiply what I already have to accomplish more in *my* community?"

The profitability of businesses depends on money-saving techniques and efficiencies. They ask, "What can we do to improve our utilization of people? How can we streamline our processes? And what can we do to elevate our products and services?"

At first glance, these questions may seem irrelevant to your particular situation. But revolutionaries also endeavor to improve, streamline, and elevate. Because waste is the enemy of change. It impedes growth and performance. Your mission suffers, people are misused, time is wasted, and resources are squandered. Every asset is vital to achieving the goal. But sitting on assets isn't the path to success. Preservation and protection are not strategies that put your resources to work; they will eventually grow stale and deteriorate. Instead, like businesses, revolutionaries constantly look for ways to multiply the quantity and quality of their assets.

You have an asset that towers above your passion, voice, finances, network, and time. It's called "your life." You have an opportunity to multiply your gifts—to make yourself a better person. The needs are so great that the world cannot afford for you to be less than your best. You have so much to offer. Beyond talents and assets, you have a deep love for people and a concern for the world. How do I know that? Because you're reading this book. Whatever you do, don't ignore the growing discontentment inside you. You know there's something more out there for you. But don't over-think it. Rather than rushing to change your vocation or location, look for opportunities to use your assets and practice disruptive compassion right where you are. That's how you live like a revolutionary.

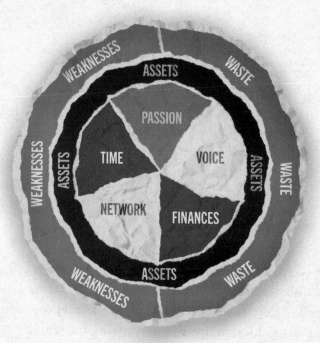

CHAPTER 5

BE AUTHENTIC

When my oldest boy was about fourteen, I started to talk to him about some of the mistakes I made in life, just to put a few dents in that shiny armor.

—Denzel Washington

My days at San Jose State were long behind me. I had discovered my sweet spot—writing magazine articles and books. Editors seemed to like my work and I was earning a solid salary. I found myself interviewing intriguing people and following the jet trails of celebrities to exotic locations—all in the name of journalism. Life was almost perfect: I was married to a beautiful woman, had two kids, and owned a tidy mortgage. But something was missing.

One morning—while pounding the keys on my laptop—the truth hit me like a linebacker sacking a quarterback. *Hal, you've escaped poverty and made a good life for yourself, but you're no longer the revolutionary who graduated from the university determined to make a difference.*

I argued against myself, recalling a host of good deeds and generous donations. But the prosecutor in my head was relentless: *You're not what you used to be. You once dreamed of helping the poor, remember?*

I countered, *Yeah, I could do more, but I still care.*

Finally, I whispered what I already knew: "Revolutionaries do more than care."

Several months passed before I boarded a plane for New York City. I told my family I was doing field research for a future book, but it was much more than that. I intended to ride shotgun with the police and conduct interviews in the streets after midnight, but this was really about reconnecting with my roots. It was time to leave my gated community and remember how the rest of the world lived.

The police sergeant sat in his windowless office in the precinct's station and clipped the end of a fresh cigar. Piles of rap sheets, reports, and photos of perpetrators competed for space on his desk. Hanging crooked on the smoke-stained wall directly behind the desk were "most wanted" posters. Two banged-up file cabinets and a leaning coatrack consumed two corners. He lit up, took a long drag on the cheap cigar, exhaled, then measured me from behind the smoke. His hollow eyes told me he was disappointed at my youth. I shifted in my seat and waited for him to speak. Instead, he rolled the cigar between his thick fingers and took another drag.

"You ever done a cop ride-along before?" he asked, not waiting for an answer. "This is New York and you're riding on the night shift."

I swallowed hard.

"Follow me," he grumbled.

I trailed him into the hallway, where he introduced me to a burly and equally brusque officer. We shook hands and made small talk. My companion for the evening was a veteran of the force, unimpressed that I would be tagging along.

With a bulletproof vest hugging my chest, we began cruising the streets. Over the radio we received orders to investigate a missing person complaint. Within minutes we pulled into "the projects"—a row of low-rent high-rise apartments. I shadowed the officer up three flights of stairs to apartment 313. The stench emanating from the apartment led us to believe there might be a dead body inside. The officer's knuckles pounded on the door.

"Police!" he shouted.

No answer.

He pounded again.

"Police! Open up."

Still no answer.

"Let's find the manager or someone who has a key," he barked in frustration.

When we struck out, the officer warned, "We're gonna have to break the door down."

I'd seen that done on television a hundred times and it always looked easy. The officer kicked the door several times. This time it didn't budge.

"Dead-bolted piece of—" he said.

He knocked on the door across the hall, which opened cautiously after a minute or two. Through the small crack I could see a sliver of poverty: uncarpeted floor, broken table, and splintered bookcase. Two children wandered around listlessly. One kid, no older than two, had urine dripping out of her soiled diaper and down her leg.

"Yeah?" said the frightened mother.

"Lookin' for the guy in 313," the officer said.

"Haven't seen him—try over there," she said.

We proceeded down the hall and banged on another door. The man who answered was nearly incoherent, one eye closed. His apartment was filled with cigarette smoke.

"You seen the fella in 313?" the officer asked, holding his breath.

"I don't know." He coughed.

"We'll go down the fire escape," the officer said as though I were his partner. "And go through the window."

He stepped onto the roof with his hand on his gun. He made sure the coast was clear before nodding for me to join him. "Roofs are a common place for drug deals to go down," he said. "You don't come waltzing out on roofs."

We scurried to the building's edge and climbed down the fire escape. When we reached the third floor, the officer smashed the window of the apartment with his flashlight and opened the pane. I stooped down behind him and stepped into an apartment shin-deep in trash: jugs, food boxes, filthy clothes, dozens of pornographic magazines, balled-up sheets, beer cans, whiskey bottles, and toilet paper.

There, under a thin sheet, was a man—alive or dead, I couldn't tell. The officer pulled back the sheet with his flashlight and the man rolled over onto his stomach. He was naked, unshaven, and in a drug-induced stupor.

The officer promptly radioed for another vehicle to transport the man to a detox facility.

"Hey," the officer called to me, "help me pick him up."

I hesitated. The smell emanating from the man on the bed was nauseating, thick and unavoidable, like warm death and sewage. I felt like I was going to vomit. I shook my head no. *It's not my job,* I told myself. *I'm not going to touch that guy.*

"Hurry up," he said, irritated.

Feeling the scorn of the officer, I complied. After cloaking him with pants and a robe, we draped his floppy arms around our necks and lugged him downstairs. With each step, my shame grew. I didn't want to get my hands dirty. I didn't want to touch him.

As the detox vehicle pulled away, I climbed into the squad car and waited for the officer to return. I stared absently at the dashboard, disappointed in myself and pondering how selfish I had become. Sitting alone, I felt as naked as the missing man. I whispered words long overdue: "God, I'm really tired of living for myself."

I helped people only when I felt impressed to do something, when it was convenient. Frankly, that made it easier to look the other way and say, "That's someone else's job." The truth was I had a lexicon of excuses to help me skirt responsibility and deal with guilt. As a kid, I saw Jesus' message as a menu to select from rather than a recipe to follow. Consequently I assembled a "fragmented Jesus" to inform and justify my actions and attitudes. But those shards offered a distorted reflection of what he really stood for. According to my misguided faith, Jesus loved those who followed him more than those who didn't. He was the Scorekeeper in the sky who awarded points for sitting through a sermon and contributing when the offering plate was passed around. As far as I was concerned, if you weren't part of a church, you were playing for the other team. Essentially, you were on your own.

But it was those very misconceptions that were holding me back from becoming a revolutionary and practicing disruptive compassion.

Merriam-Webster defines *authentic* as "conforming to an original so as to reproduce essential features." In that squad car, I finally faced the truth: if Jesus was the original, I was the fake.

Nathaniel Hawthorne said, "No man, for any considerable

period, can wear one face to himself, and another to the multitude, without finally getting bewildered as to which may be the true."[1] As Herman Melville said, "It is better to fail in originality than to succeed in imitation."[2]

I had to face the fact that true revolutionaries don't pretend to be something they're not, because impressing others isn't as important as loving them. You'll never earn the respect of your peers without authenticity. Sooner or later, they'll see who you really are.

THE JOURNEY FROM PHONY TO REAL

I found these four ideas helpful as I embarked on the journey from phony to real.

1. Be Loyal to the Truth

In his book *Zag: The Number One Strategy of High-Performance Brands*, Marty Neumeier writes, "What people want today are trustworthy brands. What they don't want is more intrusiveness, more empty claims, more clutter."[3] Let me take that one step further: Individuals are looking for trustworthy people they can believe in.

People who become revolutionaries are more loyal to the truth than they are to their cause.

At first, a phony image may appear to be harmless, but it can backfire and your credibility will suffer. The fastest way to negate disruptive compassion is through behavior or an attitude that reveals disappointing character. You can't say you love one neighbor and cheat another. You can't give a gift to one person and steal from another. Inconsistency undermines your mission. Revolutionaries, on the other hand, earn a reputation for doing the right thing and telling the truth.

Revolutionaries know exaggeration only brings grief and confusion. You don't need to embellish the facts of your life or mission to gain the support of others. If you avoid exaggeration, you won't need friends or a professional image consultant to issue a press release explaining what really happened. It's easy to fall into a pattern of saying you caught a ten-pound bass when it was actually a four pounder. What's six pounds, right?

But at some point, exaggeration becomes delusion. We assume people won't notice the inconsistencies. But they know more than we think they do. Listen, a four-pound fish is big enough—you're not trying to win the Bass Derby. Revolutionaries retain their credibility by avoiding indiscretions and exaggerations. Remember, it takes a lot less time to ruin one's credibility than to establish it.

2. Be Believable, Not Infallible

Humble people inspire others to join their cause in part because they are believable. They have a tight grip on reality. And, thank goodness, they aren't know-it-alls. They aren't afraid to say, "I don't know."

Some religious people are guilty of pretending to have an answer for every injustice. Children are malnourished, the elderly can't afford medication, and disaster victims lose their homes. Yet some are quick to say, "It must be God's will." That's code for "It's not on my radar—it doesn't affect me—I'd rather not grapple with the issue." It's those kinds of remarks and attitudes that cause critics like atheist Sam Harris to say, "It's not so much religion per se, it's false certainty that worries me."[4]

What's wrong with saying, "I don't know why children are malnourished. And quite frankly, I don't understand why women are trafficked and abused. I believe God is good and he loves everyone. But if I were sitting on his throne, I'd make sure every child had enough food and every woman was protected. Yeah, I have a long list of questions for God, but those will have to wait. Right now, he wants us to focus on saving as many lives as possible." That's being real. That's what people are searching for. They're tired of clichés and religious chatter. They want to see love in action.

Here are ten ways people know when you aren't being authentic:

1. You exaggerate when talking about yourself.
2. You let other people tell you how to think and feel.
3. You refuse to share your own opinions for fear of rocking the boat.
4. You tell people what they want to hear.
5. You don't practice what you preach.
6. You have an uneven reputation.
7. You don't treat everyone with respect.
8. You crave attention and compliments and manipulate others to get them.
9. You don't keep your promises.
10. You don't share your problems and disappointments.

3. Feel the Pain

Some believe they have to hide their pain and hardship from others. They feel compelled, for a number of reasons, to avoid any appearance of weakness. That approach may foster an image, but it won't inspire anyone. People find it difficult to relate to you if you portray that your life is problem free. What they really need to see is a revolutionary who remains focused on the mission in the midst of personal pain, setbacks, and disappointments. Someone who honestly forges ahead in the face of hardship, attacks, and injustice. That example builds courage and commitment in you and in those around you.

No one expects to see a smile on your face when you have a 103 temperature or you just watched your house burn down. "I'm doing great" just doesn't cut it. Saying "I have faith" was never a synonym for "I'm not having a hard time" or "This is easy." Get real—tell people how you feel. An occasional "I'm having a rotten day" is actually refreshing. Mother Teresa said, "Honesty and transparency make you vulnerable. Be honest and transparent anyway." Don't be afraid to show others that you are capable of being physically or emotionally hurt.

The goal is vulnerability—not invincibility. Here are four lessons for authentic living:

1. You're not a contestant on a reality TV show. You don't have to share your deepest secrets with everyone. Choose your confidants wisely. But do choose several. And share with them regularly.

2. Live in the present. Worrying about the future accomplishes nothing. Regrets are unnecessary weights and can be the most difficult to shed. What worries or regrets are holding you back from a healthier and happier life? Acknowledge them and let them go.

3. When you have a problem with something or someone, don't be afraid to deal with it head on. Don't put it off because of fear or weak conviction.

4. Be honest with yourself. Don't drum up problems because you've grown accustomed to sympathy and conflict.

4. Get Your Hands Dirty

Authentic revolutionaries are in the trenches. They are more than social media personas. They aren't afraid to break a sweat for their cause. They use their brains *and* their hands.

SOMETHING "REAL"

Seattle's Capitol Hill is the playground of thousands of teens and young adults who descend on the city from every state. Many rejected what their parents held sacred, including religion, status, and money. As children of the "grunge culture," their religion is whatever whim they choose and their sanctuary is the streets. They sit like huddled urchins on the sidewalk.

One night, I walked through Capitol Hill asking teens to share their stories. I sat on a curb next to Callie, age seventeen. She arrived in the city with her boyfriend, but when he was murdered she felt abandoned in a world that preyed upon girls like her.

"How did your boyfriend die?" I asked.

"We were leaving a party and a guy shot him."

"Why? Were they in a fight?"

"No, I don't know why it had to happen, but it did."

"What happened to the guy who shot him?"

"Don't know," she said, blank faced.

"Have you thought about going home to your parents?"

"No, I'll kill myself first. Gotta go," she said, abruptly jumping to her feet.

"Thanks for your time," I said.

She forced a smile and disappeared into the crowd.

Callie had tipped me off to a party, so along with my travel guide, we descended into a basement to check it out.

The dark-lit room and damp walls made me feel like I had entered a dungeon. Dozens of youths sucked pacifiers and lollipops to prevent them from biting their tongues in their drug-induced state. Some were slumped against walls, their heads bobbing to the amplified music. Couples were making out while others bounced on the dance floor. A guy grabbed my arm and yanked me into the gyrating mob. The music ripped through me like an electrical current.

When we finally emerged for fresh air, we bumped into a fifteen-year-old runaway named Brian. To survive, he sold his body night after night. He said he slept under cars and in alleyways. Though his voice was high-pitched, his face was hard and his eyes steel.

"How do you live?" I asked.

"I hustle."

"Where do you live?" I asked.

"Everywhere—I take care of myself."

He brandished a switchblade.

"Can you go back home to your parents?"

"They're dead," he said. "My caseworker is tryin' . . . Man, I don't want to talk about this [expletive]!"

"Anything we can do for you?" I asked.

"Got all I need. See ya."

Without warning, he bolted down the street.

"Hey, Brian," I called at his back. "Brian—wait!"

I wanted to chase after him, but I knew it was a race I couldn't win. He needed a father to wrap his arms around him and tell him he was loved. Instead, I feared he was destined to suffer the same fate as thousands before him: a life of loneliness, abuse, and emptiness, ending in a drug overdose.

What attracted Brian, Callie, and thousands more to these streets? They came looking for something real. Although I could think of safer ways to find what they were looking for, they had one thing in common: they wanted something more than what they had—something they could believe in. If they could ever find it, they'd give their lives to it.

That night, I asked more than a dozen youths to explain why they ran away from home. They said:

"My family is [messed] up!"

"I couldn't get into the materialism."

"There were too many rules at home."

"I couldn't live up to everyone's expectations."

"Our personalities were always in conflict."

"Lots of drama—so I checked out."

"They were all fakes—hypocrites."

One teenager after another said they came to Capitol Hill to find "real people" who would allow them to "be themselves." But by their own admission, they hadn't found what they were searching for. I could see the disillusionment and trepidation in their eyes. They were running alone into the vast unknown.

On my final night in Seattle, I approached a shoeless girl with tats and dreads sitting cross-legged on the sidewalk.

"How long you been comin' up here?" I asked.

She glanced up. "Why you askin'?"

"Just curious."

"A year," she replied. "But thinkin' about headin' to San Fran."

"What are you hoping to find—what are you looking for?" I asked.

"What everyone else wants—a good time."

Before I could ask her name, two of her friends invaded our conversation holding a bag of weed.

"Want to get high?" she asked.

"Can't," I replied.

"You sure? It's good stuff."

I shook my head no. But with the look of a worried parent, I said, "Please take care of yourself."

She smiled back. "You too."

I watched her cross the street and head down an alley with her friends. I leaned against a wall and surveyed the crowd. *So many stories. So much heartbreak. What will it take to unlock their potential? Perhaps it begins with them finding a revolutionary they can believe in.*

"God," I whispered, "I want to be that kind of person."

You can be that person too—an authentic revolutionary who inspires others to do great things. Jesus demonstrated that one person, led by love and kindness, can influence the lives of many. Make it your goal to influence your circle of friends and build a team that can accomplish even greater things together.

CHAPTER 6

BUILD A TEAM

A team is not a group of people who work together. A team is a group of people who trust each other.

—Simon Sinek

From a chopper, Kirk Noonan surveyed Port-au-Prince, Haiti, in disbelief. Buildings were flattened, rubble blocked streets, and makeshift tents dotted the hillside. The 7.0 earthquake had left the presidential palace and the city's main cathedral in ruins.

On the ground, rescue crews were frantically digging through the debris in search of survivors. Meanwhile, Convoy of Hope and other relief agencies had begun distributing food, water, and emergency supplies. In addition, a medical unit was established to treat the injured.

Each morning, Kirk walked the long lines leading to the triage, conversing with survivors. Many had gashes and protruding bones. One father held his lifeless daughter in his arms. "She was crushed by a wall," he said. Kirk rushed them to a doctor. A few moments later, the doctor announced, "I'm sorry—there's nothing we can do. Her injuries are too severe." With tears bathing his face, the father gently scooped his baby girl into his arms and walked away.

Kevin Rose, then a country director for Convoy of Hope in Haiti, was standing on a second-floor balcony when the earthquake struck. He narrowly escaped by racing down the stairs into the street, only to be confronted with the dead body of a young girl. He knew there wasn't time to mourn or process the trauma—the clock was ticking. Lives hung in the balance.

Kevin and the local Haitian team sprang into action, establishing points of distribution for food, water, and supplies with the help of partner organizations like the Assemblies of God, Mission of Hope, and more. Multiple shipments had arrived in-country days earlier, so he knew the warehouse was filled with emergency supplies. But nothing had prepared him for the horrors and demands of a disaster on this scale. Yet he sidelined his fears and led an initiative that kept thousands of Haitians alive.

When I landed in Port-au-Prince, Kevin and Kirk were there to meet me. As we drove toward a distribution site, Kevin said, "It's like a cloud of agony and mourning hangs over the city. People are still sleeping outside, fearful of another earthquake or tremor. They estimate that thousands of dead bodies remain inside the pancaked buildings. They're taking the bodies to a massive gravesite in the mountains."

More than a hundred thousand people were reportedly killed in the earthquake, and tens of thousands were left homeless. The stench of death hung in the air. We moved through the city in our Land Cruiser, carefully negotiating piles of rubble. Each time our vehicle came to a stand-still, panicked children knocked on the car window, their hands outstretched. I knew if I helped one, it would invite a swarm of children. But I couldn't ignore one kid's despairing eyes. I cracked the window and dropped a snack bar into his hands.

It was obvious that desperation had set in. Fires, looting, and riots had broken out across the city.

"It's going to take months for the city to stabilize and years for the nation to recover from this," Kevin said.

"Then we're going to be here a long time," I replied.

Prior to the 2010 earthquake, Convoy of Hope had launched a children's school feeding program in Haiti in partnership with another charity, Mission of Hope. A warehouse was established and delivery trucks were deployed. At the time of the earthquake, about 11,000 children were enrolled. Following the disaster, registration rose to 90,000 children, water systems were installed, schools and orphanages were built, and hundreds of farmers were trained to increase the yield of their crops. The disaster proved to be a catalyst for long-term, sustainable programs.

You can't rescue thousands of people from an earthquake on your own. And you can't feed tens of thousands of children each day with two hands, a serving spoon, and a bowl of rice and beans. Until you have a team with committed revolutionaries, you're limited to what *you* alone can accomplish. That in no way minimizes the value of individuals making disruptive compassion a personal quest. There's no denying, however, that a group of revolutionaries multiplies the potential for good.

An African proverb says, "If you want to go fast, go alone. If you want to go far, go together."[1] You want to change the world? You want to impact your neighborhood or school? Be part of a team. Whether in sports, film, family, business, or life itself, a strong supporting cast leads to greater impact. Even when compassion is delivered one person to another, there's still a team of family members and friends behind the scenes that helps to make it possible.

In the movies, even superheroes need help on occasion. When they confront a powerful nemesis, sometimes they call on reinforcements to defeat the enemy. Captain America, Black Panther, Wonder Woman, and others come to the rescue. Together they attack the enemy from different vantage points, relying on their respective superpowers. Of course, in the end, they save the world. You get the point—we're stronger together.

United acts of compassion don't just go off without a hitch on their own—they require leaders and followers. One writer said, "Teamwork [requires] very patient people, individuals who are humble, who solve problems with a high margin of diligence, with wide perspective and able to accept different opinions and sometimes admit that you were misguided and your colleague's idea was far better."[2]

Working as a team improves quality, morale, and retention. Working alone, on the other hand, reduces feedback, accountability, learning, longevity, momentum, and motivation. As one author put it, "All of this doesn't mean that working on a team is easy. We've all probably had our share of project experiences where slackers who don't pull their own weight take the fun out of teamwork. But given the . . . risks, that doesn't mean we shouldn't figure out and practice how to build effective teams."[3]

Remember George Clooney and Brad Pitt in *Ocean's Eleven*? They have a high-stakes job to rob three Las Vegas casinos simultaneously and need to recruit a team that can work together to steal millions. One small mistake will earn them jail time. So they start assembling their team, embarking on a search for white-collar thieves who can bring a unique skill set to the team. They look for reliability, loyalty, confidentiality, chemistry, and ability. And that's exactly what you need to do too. No, don't go rob a casino. Surround yourself with the right cast of characters who will join you in your mission of disruptive compassion. Find people you can count on when the stakes are high.[4]

Jesus didn't rob the Bellagio or MGM, but his mission was filled with danger and adventure. That's why he was intentional in selecting his twelve disciples. To follow him, they had to adhere to a set of rules and high expectations. It wasn't enough for them to use his name. To join, they had to take up his cause, proclaim his message, and practice disruptive compassion. He wanted them to attach their futures—their very lives—to him. He wanted them all in or not at all.

THE RIGHT PARTNERS

Your mission in life may be a personal quest to practice disruptive compassion. And that's perfectly okay. Revolutions start with someone like you. But if you choose to engage partners, they can multiply the impact of your disruptive compassion and help you reach your goals faster. These partners, for example, expanded the reach of Convoy of Hope.

TOMS and Convoy of Hope have partnered to distribute more than two million pairs of shoes to kids in need.

Another partner, the National Breast Cancer Foundation (NBCF), was established after CEO Janelle Hail won her battle with breast cancer. Since then, the organization has saved thousands of lives through its education and screening programs. NBCF has partnered with Convoy of Hope to provide breast cancer screenings and mammograms to women who have limited access.

Corporate partner Plum Organics participates in Convoy of Hope's community outreaches. Tens of thousands of guests have received nutritious super smoothies produced by Plum Organics. The company was founded on the principle that when children receive the right nutrients, they can live to their full potential and have a greater impact on the world.

Partnerships and relationships can act as anchors or accelerants. As a result, your personnel and partnership decisions will largely affect the level of influence you have in the world. If your friends are self-absorbed, those tendencies will likely become your tendencies (and probably sooner than you think). If your coworkers are generous, you'll be quick to empty your purse or wallet too. If your friends are passionate visionaries, you will be more likely to seize opportunities around you. Friendships matter. Aquaintances are more than casual accessories. They can spur you to greatness or kill your dreams before they start. Abraham Lincoln said, "I am a success today because I had a friend who believed in me and I didn't have the heart to let him down."[5]

Author Leon Logothetis said, "People have a huge impact on your life. [According to motivational speaker Jim Rohn,] 'You are the average of the five people you spend the most time with.' With this in mind, you should think about the people you're spending time with the same way you think about what you eat and how you're exercising. Some people can be parasites. They suck out your happiness, energy, and maybe some of your tangible resources as well. You can put spending time with them in the same category as eating nachos on the couch. . . . [Find] people that will inspire you to be a better person, provide you with motivation to achieve your goals, empower you to make the changes you need to succeed, and cheer on your success."[6]

Most likely you've already begun evaluating your friendships and the members of your "team." Here are five questions to help you make a fair evaluation:

1. Does this friend push you toward or pull you away from your goals?
2. Does this friend expect more from you than you want to give?
3. Does this friend add energy and inspiration to your life?
4. Does this friend add to or subtract from your momentum?
5. Does this friend make you better or worse?

Revolutionaries realize they can guard only so many flanks at one time. They need a team they can trust to share responsibility and hold one another accountable. They need people who pursue excellence, prioritize the mission, persevere in hardship, and protect the team.

PURSUE EXCELLENCE

After attending his first Convoy of Hope community outreach, Michael Redmon thought, *This is awesome, but I know we can make it even better.* And when he joined the team, he was given his chance. He began by expanding the menu of services provided and transforming the event from what resembled a food line to a carnival. Word quickly spread that Convoy of Hope knew how to "throw a party." Community leaders from across the country began calling to request a community outreach in *their* city.

When Michael was invited to speak to community leaders in Montgomery, Alabama, he studied the city's storied history. Montgomery was home to the bus boycott, Rosa Parks, and the civil rights movement. Leaders there were determined to put an end to the racial divide. But during the outreach planning process, they warned that racial tensions were rising and debated whether the event should proceed or be postponed. One pastor stood and said, "If we want to see our city change, it's gonna start with the churches coming together." That day they voted unanimously to move forward with the outreach.

A few months later, the event brought help to Montgomery. More than 1,300 volunteers—black, white, Hispanic, Asian, and more—served five thousand guests. And the mayor of Montgomery awarded Michael a key to the city. "Convoy of Hope has unlocked the heart of this city," he said. Two years later, attendance at the outreach grew to ten thousand guests.

Michael's pursuit of excellence resulted in many more families receiving help. More than 1,200 citywide events in fifty states have been conducted, mobilizing 500,000 volunteers and serving millions of honored guests.

Excellence is more likely achieved when the team is a composite of skills, passions, and personalities that operate in unity to accomplish a common mission. Every team can use a dreamer, encourager, bean counter, chaplain, broker, marketer, and manager.

PRIORITIZE THE MISSION

Prioritizing the mission doesn't have to mean sacrificing family vacations, canceling Netflix, or skipping visits to the health club. No one is asking you to give up things you love. But revolutionaries know change doesn't magically occur just because you blow out candles and make a wish. It takes a high level of commitment to fulfill your mission.

It's impossible to inspire others to be revolutionaries if you're not fired up and practicing disruptive compassion. What you do is more important than what you say. The team's level of commitment will not exceed yours. Your team or family is a reflection of you and your commitment to the mission. If you believe you've been a poor example, then take the steps to change that. Let people see a different side of you—one which shows your willingness to pay the price to change the world. It's not too late. People are watching what you do.

PERSEVERE IN HARDSHIP

Business guru Patrick Lencioni said, "Remember, teamwork begins by building trust. And the only way to do that is to overcome our need for invulnerability."[7] In other words, the know-it-all who appears to be infallible, independent, and indestructible is a phony. That person needs moral support as much as anyone. He or she is simply living in denial or hiding out of fear. Everyone experiences hardship. Everyone needs a friend. Revolutionaries are no exception. You need friends who will pray for you and build you up when it feels like the world is crashing in. Effective teams are good at encouraging one another. They fight the temptation to say, "That's their problem," or, "That's not my area." When one person struggles, the team struggles and accepts the challenge to pick him or her up.

Nobody wants to belong to a team of quitters. When times are difficult, revolutionaries are determined to complete the task. Regardless of the time requirement, sacrifice, or hardship, you are committed to your mission. Be the one who stands up and says, "We're not done yet—we can do this." Yeah, I know that sounds a bit cheesy, like a line from *Mission Impossible*. But sometimes it just needs to be said.

A great team will help you remember why you're doing this and underscore that you're in it together.

PROTECT THE TEAM

Revolutionaries protect their team members (family, friends, and mission partners). They recognize the contributions of each member and work hard to keep them moving in the same direction. Business icon Henry Ford said, "Coming together is a beginning. Keeping together is progress. Working together is success."[8]

Various attitudes and behaviors can erode team chemistry: envy, selfishness, ambition, inflexibility, poor conflict resolution, and more. That's why the Bible says, "Be devoted to one another in love. Honor one another above yourselves" (Rom. 12:10). It's hypocritical to say you're all for disruptive compassion, then turn around and blast a team member. That's not how you build a solid team, nor is it the kind of disruption we're shooting for.

Kindness does not mean sweeping problems under the rug either. When Judas fell out of step with the other disciples,

Jesus confronted him about his attitude and priorities. (See John 13:21–30.) Judas wasn't satisfied being on the team—he wanted to call the shots and turn their mission into a profitable venture. He was given a chance to change his attitude. Instead, he betrayed Jesus and the team for thirty pieces of silver. Ultimately, the guilt associated with his actions cost him his life. At times you may be the one who needs to speak truth in kindness to a team or family member. Other times you will be the one who needs to receive truth with grace and humility. Phil Jackson, an NBA legend, said, "The strength of the team is each individual member. The strength of each member is the team."[9]

In 2016, Hurricane Matthew sliced through Haiti, killing more than five hundred people and causing more than $1 billion in damage. Food, water, and emergency supplies were in urgent need. BNSF Railway offered to help Convoy of Hope respond to the need by transporting meals by train from Missouri to Florida. From there, containers would be shipped to Haiti and our partner, Mission of Hope. There was only one challenge for our supply-chain team and its leader, Erick Meier: they had to deliver twelve million meals "immediately."

"We can do it!" Erick said, even though he realized he was signing his team up for a monumental task. The next forty-eight hours proved to be a masterful display of teamwork and logistics. The supply-chain team worked around the clock. As a result, twelve million life-sustaining meals were delivered to survivors in Haiti right on schedule. "We showed what can be accomplished when you have a team that's more concerned about getting the job done than getting credit," Eric said. "Everyone did their job—and sacrificed sleep—without complaint because we believed in the mission."

At the heart of any successful team is a group of people who are united behind a common desire to practice disruptive compassion. The cause or revolution isn't about them. No one lives for power and praise. They're motivated by the mission of putting smiles on faces. They genuinely care more for others than themselves, and that's the secret to any team's success.

CHAPTER 7

PAY THE INVOICE

It's when you're acting selflessly that you are at your bravest.

—Veronica Roth

Maybe it's time for us to do something else," I said to my wife, Doree. "The mission of Convoy of Hope is right, but I just . . ." I paused and let out a sigh, contemplating my next words carefully. "I don't think we can keep it going much longer." She looked back at me, her eyes admitting she knew the same. "We're tired, our credit card is maxed out," I continued, "and I'm away from you and the kids too much. Unless something happens really soon, it's going to be time for us to move on."

"We've come so far and given so much to it. God needs to show us what to do," she replied, her voice teetering between faith and desperation.

I didn't want to quit, but the personal cost was mounting. To keep it together, I quoted Scripture to myself: "Let us not grow weary of doing good, for in due season we will reap, if we do not give up" (Gal. 6:9 ESV). Nevertheless, I felt more and more alone, despite the support I had around me. Doree, my brothers, my sister, and my friends believed in the vision and were making their own sacrifices to see the fledgling organization succeed. I didn't want to let anyone down. I couldn't. But I began to doubt whether I had the ability to lead any longer. *Maybe I was born to do something else,* I told myself.

Randy Rich and his wife, Lisa, were close friends of ours who had left their jobs to join the mission. Randy had been serving on staff at a local church when he woke up one night with a gut intuition that a change was coming. A few days later, I invited him and Lisa to join our small team. There was only one problem: we didn't have enough to pay either of them an adequate salary. Nevertheless they came, without health insurance, paid vacations, retirement, or other benefits. Randy was the architect of the first outreaches, and Lisa managed the office. Given all they had sacrificed, I dreaded the day I'd have to tell them I was quitting. I didn't know the exact timeline, but the clock was ticking and hope was waning.

One afternoon, driving alone in my car, I made a promise to God and myself: "Something has to happen in the next few weeks—by the time we hold the Convoy of Hope outreach in Fresno—or I'm done. I'll go find a journalism job and take care of my family, and someone else can do this."

It wasn't a casual threat. I was serious.

The sun's rays were relentless that day in Fresno, California, but that didn't discourage the guests. Several thousand stood in line for hours before the gates opened. When "go time" came, hundreds of trained volunteers were on hand ready to serve guests meals and provide medical and dental screenings, job opportunities, haircuts, and more. The smiles on everyone's faces told the story—the event was a huge success. Families enjoyed quality time together; kids got their faces painted; and individuals were connected to programs and churches to help them escape poverty. Mission accomplished. But no one knew the battle being waged inside my head.

How can you even consider walking away from all these hurting families? I scolded myself. *What if today never happened?*

I countered, *Yeah, but we've done our part. We helped get it started. Someone else can take it from here.*

My debate was interrupted by a handshake. "You have a big crowd out here today," the man said.

"Yes, we're expecting five thousand guests, and I believe we may surpass that," I replied. "Thanks for coming out."

I had met Bob Clay and his wife, Rosa, once before. Their son, Rob, was a good friend and Convoy of Hope volunteer. I knew the family owned a business and traveled extensively, so I was surprised to see Bob helping at the outreach that day. Handing me an envelope, he said, "I wanted to give you this."

"Thank you. Should I open it now or later?"

"It's up to you," he said.

I slid my finger under the seal and glimpsed the corner of what looked like a check. I peered inside to find a donation of $25,000 and a handwritten note that said: "God is with you—keep going." My jaw dropped. I stood in stunned silence for a few moments as tears streamed down my face. This was the sign I had been looking for.

I couldn't even say "Thank you." I could only sob and nod with gratitude.

Bob smiled and said, "You're welcome—use it where you need it most."

I wanted to throw my arms around him and tell him how

this was the answer to my prayers. This was a miracle. But that gesture would have to wait until later. At that moment, I politely excused myself and drifted behind a tree to bury my face in my hands and cry alone. I was thankful for the incredible gift, but the amount wasn't what moved me most. It was as if God himself had written that note. It was his way of speaking directly to the situation we found ourselves in. We knew now we had to keep going, because the adventure was just beginning. As it turns out, sometimes the only thing standing between us and success is patience, perseverance, and simple faith in the midst of overwhelming doubt.

Many people paid a price to launch and sustain Convoy of Hope. It never would have survived without extraordinary sacrifice. We learned that giving hope to people is not expensive—but neither is it free. It requires people like you choosing a life of generosity so others can have a life of opportunity. Revolutionaries understand that. They aren't on a quest for personal comfort. They don't give to get—they give to give. Movements thrive and change occurs because revolutionaries are willing to "pay the invoice." They invest their lives and resources without the promise of victory or a guaranteed rate of return. They give because they know the cause has no hope if someone doesn't stand up and declare, "I'll do whatever it takes."

At the community outreaches, I like to stand at the entrance and greet guests as they arrive. So much can be communicated when you look someone in the eye and show them honor with a smile and a handshake. At the same time, it's disheartening to see so many families living day-to-day, desperate for help. Many of the children need new shoes and backpacks for school. The parents, meanwhile, need to consult a doctor or dentist or receive help preparing their résumé.

So many heartbreaking stories of lost jobs, health problems, and misfortune. I can empathize to a degree because my childhood family was also a victim of circumstances. We only escaped poverty because people were willing to make sacrifices (to pay the invoice) on our behalf.

On a larger scale, Convoy of Hope's volunteers and donors are paying the invoice for impoverished children and families around the world. They refuse to let famine, poverty, and tragedy stand in the winner's circle. They reject the notion the battle has already been lost. They practice disruptive compassion, because they believe their sacrifices can translate into changed lives, and changed lives can lead to a better world.

GENEROSITY DEFINED

According to *Guinness World Records*, the word *set* has the most meanings in the English language.[1] In the *Oxford English Dictionary*, it has 430 meanings and also boasts the longest entry, coming in at a whopping 60,000 words and 326,000 characters. It's understandably hard, then, to simply define *set*. But if we throw around words like *mission*, *compassion*, *faith*, and *generosity*, we're not always sure what they mean. There aren't hundreds of definitions for these terms, but we tend to define them based on our own experiences.

The University of Notre Dame College of Arts and Letters set out to answer one simple question: "What is generosity?"[2] The word is derived from Latin, they said, and had the original meaning "of noble birth." During the seventeenth century, the definition began to shift toward "of noble spirit." It signified one who possessed the ideals of nobility: courage, strength, and fairness. In the eighteenth century, generosity came to represent open-handedness—the giving of one's money and possessions to others.

The study ultimately answered its research question by defining generosity as "the virtue of giving good things to others freely and abundantly. . . . In a world of moral contrasts, generosity entails not only the moral good expressed but also many vices rejected (selfishness, greed, fear, meanness). . . . What exactly generosity gives can be various things: money, possessions, time, attention, aid, encouragement, emotional availability, and more."[3]

Author Joshua Becker said, "By definition, true generosity requires a level of contentment. It recognizes the reality that giving our resources to another person means we have less for ourselves. In this way, contentment forms the foundation for generosity. But in response, surprisingly enough, generosity also becomes the fuel for greater contentment."[4]

When generosity becomes a part of your DNA, it doesn't just affect what you do with your assets; it affects how you think and how you see the world. Consider, for example, the following ways generous people might have a different vantage point:

- They reject the scarcity mindset, seeing resources where others see none.
- Their default setting is to believe the best, not expect the worst.
- They unashamedly pursue more resources so they can do more for others.
- They believe the size of the gift is less important than the heart behind it.
- They operate from a place of gratitude, not entitlement.

According to an article in *Time* magazine, being generous really does make you happier. Researchers discovered that merely thinking about doing something generous has positive benefits in the brain.

In a new study published in *Nature Communications*, researchers from the University of Zurich in Switzerland told 50 people they'd be receiving about $100 over a few weeks. Half of the people were asked to commit to spending that money on themselves, and half were asked to spend it on someone they knew. The researchers wanted to see whether simply pledging to being generous was enough to make people happier. So before doling out any money, they brought everyone into the lab and asked them to think about a friend they'd like to give a gift to and how much they would hypothetically spend. They then performed functional MRI scans to measure activity in three regions of the brain associated with social behavior, generosity, happiness, and decision making.

Their choices—and their brain activity—seemed to depend on how they had pledged to spend the money earlier. Those who had agreed to spend money on other people tended to make more generous decisions throughout the experiment, compared to those who had agreed to spend it on themselves. They also had more interaction between the parts of the brain associated with altruism and happiness, and they reported higher levels of happiness after the experiment was over.[5]

GENEROSITY BURNOUT

If you've contributed to a charity, you're likely on someone's mailing list. You're among the millions who receive regular field reports and requests for donations. If you're on twenty or thirty mailing lists, you probably feel like you're being deluged with information. That has contributed to generosity burnout. But there are certainly a myriad of reasons for compassion fatigue. Here are a few steps you can take to avoid burnout:

1. Don't give out of obligation alone.
2. Learn to say "I can't" or "not now."
3. Give to causes that interest you.
4. Donate to people and organizations you can trust implicitly.
5. Don't limit yourself to institutional giving.
6. Give directly to individuals God places in your path.
7. Include your children in the giving process.
8. Make it a priority to support the work of your church.
9. Look for creative ways to multiply your giving.

GIVERS, GATHERERS, AND GOERS

Nothing lasts without a solid foundation. For Convoy of Hope, the foundation consists of core values and a common mission shared by generous donors, volunteers, and team members. The organization is a composite of revolutionaries: the givers—those who fuel the engine; the gatherers—those who build the network; and the goers—the hands and feet on the ground.

Revolutionary givers see their hard-earned resources not as theirs to squander but rather as theirs to spend wisely or steward well. They may work sixty-hour weeks so they can give more away. They walk the walk: "Don't hoard treasure down here. . . . Stockpile treasure in heaven" (Matt. 6:19–20 MSG).

Revolutionary gatherers are also vital to any movement. They have a gift for collecting resources to fulfill the mission. But they go beyond that. They also expand the network through advocacy and recruitment.

Students at University of Missouri's Chi Alpha group are gatherers. Under the guidance of directors Tom and Missi Trask, the students raised $42,000 in one month for feedONE, a campaign that supports Convoy of Hope's Children's Feeding Program. Students held a variety of fundraisers on campus: "For $5, swing a sledgehammer at my car." "For $2, pet my dog." "For $10, compete in a dodgeball tournament." They know how to gather!

Mark and Irma Cortez are also revolutionary gatherers. Their daughter, Kristi, was sixteen when she passed away from pneumonia and scoliosis. She was blind and couldn't walk, but she was quick to laugh and flash a smile. She brought lots of joy to her family and friends. Following her death, Mark and Irma wanted to establish something in her memory. With the help of their church, they launched an annual golf tournament, which has provided hundreds of thousands in contributions to feed hungry children around the world.

Revolutionary goers are on the front lines, distributing supplies, caring for the sick, feeding the hungry, and training mothers and farmers. Convoy of Hope mobilizes tens of thousands of workers and volunteers each year to meet needs.

Together, revolutionary givers, gatherers, and goers pay a price so others can find hope.

Exiting the 747 jetliner in Khartoum, Sudan, my shoes felt like they melted the moment I touched the tarmac. It was 117 degrees, and I was there to write a story on the refugee crisis. Reportedly, more than 700,000 people were at risk, and an estimated two million had already died over the years from war, famine, and disease. Displacement rates were astronomical, with five million people forced to flee their homes. It was an ongoing tragedy that much of the world had overlooked.

The following day, our guide led our film crew and me atop a hotel to take photographs and B-roll footage of the city's landscape and the impressive Nile River. We disregarded our taxi driver's warning not to take pictures or travel outside the city until we obtained a government permit. Poor decision. I was interviewing our guide when five soldiers with rifles stormed the roof. Instinctively I tucked my recording device in my underwear. (I was born for espionage.) They shouted and brandished their weapons.

"They're telling us to raise our hands and surrender our cameras," the guide said. "Your passports too."

We complied, but they weren't satisfied with that. The barrel of a rifle jabbed into my back as they escorted us downstairs. I could just hear Oprah's voice in my head saying, "Don't let them take you to a second location."

"Where are they taking us?" I asked.

"To their commander," the guide whispered. "Be careful what you say." His warning did nothing to assuage my alarm. *Next time we'll get a permit*, I told myself.

Once we reached our destination, one by one we were taken to interrogation rooms and locked inside with a soldier.

"Who sent you?" he demanded in broken English.

"We came to help the refugees."

"No, who sent you?" he repeated.

"American press—we came to bring attention to the refugees." I had hardly finished my statement when he pointed and said, "CIA!"

I handed him my press badge. "No—the press."

"CIA."

"Press."

The volley and grilling lasted an hour, until finally he flung open the door and motioned for me to leave. I rejoined the team and we quickly gathered our passports and cameras and fled the building.

An hour later, we entered a refugee camp to rendezvous with a UN representative. He said water sources in western Sudan had dried up and food prices had skyrocketed. "Many are surviving on roots and leaves, and meningitis is spreading," he said. He rolled out a map and showed us where fighting continued to rage between government forces and recessionist groups. "Missionaries and relief workers have also been targeted in these areas. They're putting their own lives at risk but have chosen to ignore evacuation orders."

The camp was a maze of mud-brick dwellings. No shade trees, no running water, no electricity. It was a dust bowl. It was hard to fathom: an estimated two million people were living in settlements just like this one.

"Why have you chosen to stay?" I asked the rep, my shirt soaked in perspiration.

"I don't see an end to this crisis anytime soon," he said. "How can I sit back and watch people die?"

I asked a missionary working in the camp the same question. He and his family had given years of their lives in the country. "We came initially," he shared, "because Christians were being killed and displaced because of their faith. We had to do something to help them."

As though scrolling through Instagram, my mind raced from image to image of relief workers, missionaries, social workers, and church members who were "paying the invoice" to help people in need. They were disrupting the status quo with selflessness and generosity. It made me think about Luke 6:38 (MSG): "Give away your life; you'll find life given back, but not merely given back—given back with bonus and blessing. Giving, not getting, is the way. Generosity begets generosity."

In a remote village in the mountains of El Salvador, I met a pastor and his wife who were "paying the invoice" for children and single mothers. Each week they made a two-hour drive to feed and educate children and provide job training to mothers.

"How many days are you here each week?" I inquired.

"Four or five days," the woman said.

"I don't see housing—where do you sleep?"

The pastor pointed to the back of their pickup truck. I peered past it, figuring there must be some structure in the background that I couldn't see. Scanning, I realized there was nothing.

"The truck?" I asked.

"*Sí*," he answered brightly.

"You drive back and forth every week?" I wanted to be sure I understood correctly.

"*Sí*," he said, nodding.

"How do you bathe?" I asked. "I notice there's no running water."

"Bucket and soap," the wife said.

"What motivates you to pay such a great price every week?" I asked.

"Because this is what Jesus would do," she said. "We don't have money to give, so we give our lives." Her answer made the model of my car and the size of my home insignificant. It made my worries about a hotel room that night seem trivial.

My friend Randy Hurst accompanied me to a Convoy of Hope community outreach. On the day he decided to visit, temperatures plummeted and it began to drizzle. Many of the guests were unprepared for the cold. Noticing a shivering teenager wearing only a T-shirt, Randy removed his expensive leather jacket without hesitation and draped it around the young man.

"This is for you," Randy said. "Stay warm."

It was two sizes too large, but the kid didn't mind. To him it was more valuable than a tailored tuxedo. "Thank you," he said. "I'll give it back . . . when I leave."

"No, I want you to have it," Randy said. "It looks good on you."

The teen smiled, revealing crooked teeth and a charming grin. "Thanks, man, really," he said.

That moment—that single interaction—triggered something magical. Other volunteers began taking off their jackets and giving them to coatless guests. Pretty soon it was the volunteers and not the guests who were shivering, but they did so with frozen smiles. They showed that love and kindness still exist. Disruptive compassion is contagious, and when you pay the price for someone, it inspires others to give as well.

Revolutionaries pay the invoice for disruptive compassion,

but often they don't do it alone. When observing our dedication to a mission, our family members and friends often make sacrifices right along with us. While working on his master's degree in journalism, Kirk Noonan compiled his portfolio to begin the dreaded job hunt. One morning at 3:00 he couldn't sleep and began reviewing his writing samples. Angry and frustrated that his work wasn't good enough, he began shredding page after page until a snowdrift appeared on the living room floor. Tiring, he returned to bed, questioning his ability as an aspiring writer and doubting his future entirely. The following morning, he shuffled his way to the living room to find his wife, Janna, kneeling over the pile of scrapped prose. Scotch tape in hand, she was carefully reassembling the pages one shred at a time.

When you enlist family members and friends to join you in your mission, they become crucial to your success. They're the first ones to say, "Press on—don't give up," when you feel like quitting. They offer encouragement when you need it most. Through this experience, Kirk was reminded that he and Janna were on this adventure together. This was her mission as much as it was his. They were both ready to pay the price, take risks, and face challenges to make a difference in the world.

Revolutionaries choose to invest in other people. They see value where others see none. They believe every individual is precious and worthy of an investment. And they believe everyone has something to invest.

FOUR WAYS TO GIVE

Revolutionaries practice disruptive compassion, utilizing a wide range of currencies, including possessions, time, words, and help. Let's take a look at these four ways you can give.

1. Give Your Possessions

One afternoon I was inspired to research closet organization techniques and came across one that was particularly intriguing. You put every item on a hanger and turn it so the end of the hook faces you. When you pull an item out of the closet to wear it, simply flip the hanger the other way around. At the end of a season, you know which articles of clothing to donate to a charity by noting which hangers were never turned around.

Unfortunately I didn't complete the exercise. Instead I look at my closet and repeatedly ask myself, *Why do I keep these clothes? Why won't I just give them to someone who could actually use them?* The truth is I *am* willing to give them away, but here's the problem: it takes effort. It requires me to interrupt the rest of my day long enough to sort through what I don't wear and transfer what I don't need to someone else. Again—not expensive, but not free. Not complicated, but not automatic. The same is true of our other resources. Often we don't stop long enough to ask, "What do I really need? What do I have to give away?" Famed preacher John Wesley said, "Having, first, gained all you can, and, second, saved all you can, then give all you can."[6]

Consider conducting an inventory of your life. List all the stuff you own, and keep track of what you are actually using. Then explore ways to repurpose what you don't need to benefit someone else. Give to a friend. Donate. Lend. Sell and donate proceeds. Recycle. Upcycle. Teach a kid how to play that violin you've had collecting dust in your garage. The opportunities are endless.

2. Give Your Time

"Time is money." Okay, sure, but some people don't actually need your money. They need your time. Quality time is one of the five love languages for a reason.[7] Spending time with someone sends the message that you care, that the other person has worth. And believe it or not, you don't have to apply for a work visa and travel to El Salvador or Sudan to practice this one. There are people in your own small part of the hemisphere who just need to hear someone say "you matter" with more than words, money, or things. You have the power to transform the way people see themselves, just by spending thirty minutes over a cup of coffee. Don't believe me? Try it. Extend an invitation to someone in your workplace, neighborhood, school, or church. My guess is you'll be surprised by all the good that can be accomplished with just a small portion of your time.

3. Give Encouraging Words

At one time or another, everyone feels the sting of words. Perhaps you were bullied, accused of something you didn't do, or victimized by gossip and jealousy. You know that if you retaliate, a war of words will ensue and your own bitterness will grow. Words can be weapons, but they can also be welcome mats. You know, those small rugs with flowers and phrases outside of homes that extend an invitation, that suggest a place is friendly, that say, "You're not going to be turned away." A kind and thoughtful word has the same effect. It has the power to invite, heal, and restore.

Pick a day this week and keep track of your interactions with people. For each conversation, evaluate whether your words were a welcome mat or a do not disturb sign. Did your words invite, help, and heal, or did they distance, damage, or demean? Be honest with yourself. Once you've identified any instances when your words weren't constructive, drill down on the reasons and vow to do better.

4. Give Help

If you encounter a person in need and don't show them kindness, it's possible no one will. A helping hand is often all it takes to restore a person's hope. That may mean defending a coworker who is being mocked by others. Maybe it's reporting an injustice you've witnessed. Or perhaps it's helping a person in the grocery line who comes up a few bucks short. Whatever the situation, find the courage to help. Next time you catch yourself hoping someone else will step in, be the one who does.

When you find yourself with five or ten minutes to spare, pull up a note on your phone and jot "Help Wanted" at the top. List the times when you needed help, but no one came to the rescue: your car wouldn't start, your phone was lost, or you were caught in a downpour without an umbrella. No fun. Then consider all the times when help arrived just in time: a ride to work, a visit in the hospital, a bag of groceries. When disruptive compassion is a major part of your lifestyle, you seize opportunities like these to help people in need.

After delivering a speech at a conference, I was escorted off the platform by the host. Without warning, a woman charged down the aisle toward me. I couldn't read whether she was coming to hug me or hit me. But as she approached, I noticed her dress was two sizes too large and her sandals were tattered. She threw her arms open and wrapped them around my neck just before pushing two dollars into my hand. "Please use this to feed a hungry child," she whispered. "Will you do that for me?"

"Yes, thank you," I replied.

As the woman retreated to her seat, the host turned to me and said, "Hal, I'm sure she gave you all she had. We're trying to help her get off the streets. She's homeless."

Instantly I felt ashamed for noticing her attire. She had just made an incredible sacrifice—greater than anything I'd done—and I was focused on her wardrobe. I told myself, *I can't accept a donation from a homeless woman. I just can't. I should be the one giving her money.* But then I caught myself. *That would be disrespectful and dishonoring of her. She gave because she wanted to be generous. To her, that's all that matters. Who am I to tell her she can't "pay the invoice" for a hungry child?* All I knew to do was pray that God would reward her kindness and give her a place to lay her head.

CHAPTER 8

CREATE MOMENTUM

*I think the tiniest little thing can change the
course of your day, which can change the course of
your year, which can change who you are.*

—Taylor Swift

New Orleans is underwater—we're headed in," Kary Kingsland said. As the point person for Convoy of Hope's disaster services team, he had deployed his team and staged tractor trailers filled with supplies to the region before Hurricane Katrina even made landfall. Little did he know that he and his team would spend the next two years helping citizens in Louisiana, Mississippi, and Alabama put their lives back together. Katrina, a Category 5 hurricane, caused more than $195 billion in damage and killed 1,833 people.[1] Convoy of Hope responded by sending nearly a thousand tractor-trailer loads of food, water, and supplies, along with debris removal and "mudout" crews.

Our disaster services team has responded to hundreds of disasters around the world, including the 9/11 attack on the

Twin Towers, the Joplin tornado, and Typhoon Haiyan. But the deployment to Hurricane Jeanne, in 2004, was among the most memorable. A point of distribution was established in Port Saint Lucie, Florida. Hardly any time passed before the line of cars waiting for emergency food, water, and supplies stretched a mile long. As our site leader was managing the operation, he was approached by two men who looked like they had stepped off the set of *Men in Black*. They announced they were part of President George W. Bush's security team. The very next day, President Bush and his entourage visited the site and began passing out supplies right alongside our team, shoulder to shoulder. As you might imagine, the motorists were surprised to find the president of the United States handing them bottles of water. Then, surrounded by television cameras, the president addressed the nation standing smack dab in front of a Convoy of Hope tractor trailer.

That moment, according to some, catapulted the organization. But that moment did not materialize on its own—it was the result of the team's grit and drive year after year. It was the culmination of years of meeting needs when no one was watching and no one knew the name Convoy of Hope. From the very beginning, our disaster services team didn't talk about what they hoped to do; they just did it. They didn't wait until they owned trucks and managed warehouses filled with supplies. They did all they could with borrowed trucks and leased storage space. It was that commitment, that willingness to go as fast and as far as possible with what they had, that paved the way for a catalytic moment like the arrival of a president.

Catalytic moments are like a match; they can ignite a massive fire or flicker out in seconds. When these moments of opportunity come, you must be prepared to capitalize on them and ride the waves of momentum they create. But at the same time, many movements have died because they were built solely on a singular moment everyone assumed would last. History tells us that catalytic moments are great for generating enthusiasm, but only for a season. When moments don't evolve into movements, the voices of supporters become hoarse, feet grow weary, and attention fades. The excitement expires. That's why revolutionaries need to understand the critical role of momentum and how to harness it.

Chasing momentum is different from *creating* momentum. You don't chase momentum like it's a swath of unleashed helium balloons, running haphazardly after every idea and opportunity, hoping for a breakthrough. For businesses and charities, that only leads to mission drift, compromise, and confusion among your team and supporters. Creating momentum is more calculated and under your control. You evaluate a moment and determine if and how your mission can capitalize on the opportunities it creates. Then you invest resources strategically. Momentum is created when you successfully build upon a catalytic moment.

Momentum is the tendency of an object to keep moving in the same direction, and when an object has a lot of momentum, it's difficult to change its direction. Former Secretary General of the United Nations Ban Ki-moon described progress this way: "We might liken it to riding a bicycle. You stay upright and move forward so long as you keep up the momentum." It's the revolutionary's job to keep pedaling and to encourage others to do the same. Together they can build speed that's difficult to stop.

The critical element is visible progress. Not explosive progress—just visible. Every revolution needs momentum to remain a movement. How many times have you started—and then quit—a fad diet, exercise routine, or study schedule? Sure, you began with enthusiasm but gave up because it just wasn't working. Movements die for the same reason. Incremental progress is critical to sustaining a movement.

In an interview, a journalist asked me to explain Convoy of Hope's momentum. I replied, "When we see needs, we simply ask, 'What can we do?' While bureaucrat types and others debate strategies and parcel out blame and responsibility, we accept our role, and that's to simply respond to the need." Action is central to progress, momentum, and credibility.

If you're like me, you gravitate to formulas in life because they're easier to follow. Unfortunately, momentum is less about following a formula and more about having stamina. In other words, will you keep shoveling when the ground is hard? Will you keep speaking out when people say you should be silent? Will you keep giving when you feel you have nothing more to give? Momentum is impossible without a determination that says, "My muscles ache and my face is sunburned, but I'm staying glued to my surfboard until the next big wave comes."

HOW TO HARNESS MOMENTUM

Here are ten principles for turning moments into movements, harnessing momentum, and making that momentum more predictable and sustainable.

1. Choose a Symbol

Every successful movement uses symbols and icons to draw people to their cause. They find a person, object, theme, or event that aligns with their mission. The symbol can be a politician, religious leader, philosopher, advocate, martyr, or victor. Other times, the symbol is a significant object, a seismic event, or a genre of music that people rally around, such as the Statue of Liberty, Selma's civil rights marches, or Nirvana's hit song "Smells Like Teen Spirit."

Sometimes revolutionaries become indistinguishable from their cause. *They* become the symbol. Jesus, for example, burst onto the scene with disruptive compassion, and before long, his name represented a compassion movement. Mahatma Gandhi and Nelson Mandela became symbols of the quest for freedom. And musicians like Kurt Cobain or the Beatles became symbols of rebellion.

Gandhi's revolution, for example, spread quickly because of his unwavering dedication. But he also used a symbol called "the charkha" to make his case. It was a spinning wheel used to create Indian clothing. To gain independence from Great Britain, Gandhi urged his fellow citizens to make their own clothing rather than purchase British imports. Photographs of Gandhi with a charkha became a symbol of defiance and self-sufficiency for India. And ultimately, India gained independence in 1947.[2]

When the South African government introduced apartheid in 1948, Mandela organized nonviolent demonstrations. Arguably, it was his writings and photographs of his incarceration that broke the back of apartheid. He served twenty-seven years in prison, where he became a symbol of government oppression and injustice. His release in 1990 sparked an international celebration. And in 1994, Mandela was elected president.

Icons (which are frequently an extension of a symbol) also play a factor in our everyday decisions. Where we work, play, eat, shop, and live are largely influenced by images and personalities created by Madison Avenue branding gurus. For example, you entered a drive-thru because you caught a glimpse of the Golden Arches. You used Priceline to book a hotel because you remembered a commercial featuring actress Kaley Cuoco. You cast a yes vote because you read a catchy slogan on a campaign poster. Icons and slogans have the power to influence our behavior and attitudes.

Make sure the symbols you choose represent who you are, what you value, and whom you want to help. (If you're struggling to identify your symbol, pay attention to the next chapter's advice on getting focused and eliminating distraction.)

2. Protect Your Name

I recognized his face, but I was a little surprised by his faded jeans, flannel shirt, and cowboy boots. Like most Americans, I'd only seen him in a suit and tie. I was waiting for a table in a restaurant outside Jacksonville, Florida, when he extended his hand and said, "Hello, I'm Billy Graham."

"Nice to meet you," I said in disbelief.

Immediately his name meant something: integrity, believability, and sincerity. He was in Florida to receive cancer treatments at the Mayo Clinic, so I was impressed that he took time to greet a stranger. Obviously he wasn't playing the role of a victim. His handshake was firm and his smile genuine.

Whether you know it or not, your name also means something. You're a symbol of *something* to *someone*. Your momentum and influence will only be as strong as the meaning of your name. Even the strongest momentum and most profound influence can be undermined or nullified if your character is questionable and your name marred. If you have a bad reputation, you won't be trusted. And without trust, your potential for good is minimized. That doesn't mean you should go out and try to create a persona. Anyone with access to a computer can do that. This isn't about building an image. It's about earning a reputation, not creating one.

People will follow a charismatic leader for a season; they will follow a revolutionary with character for a lifetime. Momentum begins when you become who you say you are. It begins in you. You don't beat your chest and say, "Look at me." Instead, bang the drum and yell, "These people need our help—together let's put an end to this injustice!"

Generally, revolutionaries aren't self-promoters. They let their actions and achievements speak for themselves. There is nothing wrong with name recognition—as long as you don't use it for yourself. A good name goes a long way toward accomplishing positive outcomes.

3. Go Positive

I know I'm not the only one who loathes negative political advertisements, regardless of their party affiliation. I have my finger on the mute button during election season. And yet, through extensive research, marketers have proven that negative messages can be effective in building momentum: "Don't vote for that candidate—he's a crook." "Don't buy their clothes—they're cheap." "Don't eat at that restaurant—it will make you fat." We've become accustomed to negative talking points and images. But author John Centofanti noted two dangers of using negative symbols and messages: First, you're associating negativity with your cause or brand. Second, if your product or service is so great—or your cause is so important—why show signs of desperation by going negative?[3]

Some leaders see other charities, churches, or civic organizations as competitors. They're in an imaginary contest for financial resources, publicity, and volunteers. So they're quick to criticize one another, pointing out why they are better and more deserving than the competition. But that perspective is shortsighted. I remember being approached by a major news network to appear on national television and criticize another charity. Obviously I declined. When people ask me to explain what makes Convoy of Hope superior to other charities, I offer the same answer: "I don't know the inner workings of other organizations, but I know Convoy of Hope. Here's what we're doing." To answer that question any other way hurts our reputation and theirs. Build momentum by choosing to remain positive.

4. Lead with Heart and Hard Work, Not Hype

Movements can't survive on hype. They require diligence, passion, and productivity. Hype uses loud words but has nothing to back it up. Heart and hard work, on the other hand, shout credibility.

During a training session at his car dealership, the owner told his sales team, "We need you to sell cars, but I don't want you overselling them. Just tell customers what you'd want a salesperson to tell you." Talk about refreshing! He was asking them to tone down the hype and sell with their hearts. "In the long run," he said, "if customers feel they can trust you, they'll come back time and again." He was more interested in building his business the right way—for the long haul—than selling a few more cars in the short term using manipulative tactics. Martial artist Bruce Lee said it this way: "Long-term consistency beats short-term intensity."[4]

Author Anthony Moore said, "Most people rely on short,

intense bursts of inspiration and motivation in their attempts to be successful. Maybe they read an inspiring weight-loss story, or just watched *Gladiator*. After this inspiration, they act like a crazy person—they work tirelessly, day and night. They go to the gym six days in a row for two weeks, they write five thousand words for their book, they throw out every piece of junk food they have in their house. But what usually happens to these people? The same fate that befalls nearly 92 percent of individuals who make New Year's Resolutions: they give up a couple weeks later. Enthusiasm is common. Endurance is rare."[5]

Actor Will Smith, when asked about the keys to his success, said, "The only thing that I see that is distinctly different about me is I'm not afraid to die on a treadmill. I will not be outworked, period. You might have more talent than me, you might be smarter than me, you might be sexier than me, you might . . . got it on me in nine categories. But if we get on the treadmill together, there's two things: You're getting off first, or I'm going to die."[6]

Jesus wasn't lazy either. He didn't own a treadmill, but he likely wore out a few pairs of sandals along the way. He accomplished his task because he woke up every morning determined to make his day count. (And, yes, Jesus did sleep.) He wasn't into hype. He often had to dial back his disciples who would have recruited thousands of Facebook friends and created an Instagram account. Their website would have contained photos of Jesus standing next to the blind man, the leper, the adulteress, and more. And certainly they would have given the public an opportunity to make an online donation. If they had their way, Jesus' photo would have been everywhere. When you read the Bible, you never get the sense he sought publicity for the sake of publicity. It was all about the mission, and he was a master at reminding his team of their objectives. He wasn't afraid of fame, but he wanted the kind of recognition that led to changed lives. His mission went far beyond building a fan club that clamored for his autograph. He didn't come to entertain. He came to save the world. He wanted more than their adulation—he wanted their hearts and lives.

Revolutionaries are like magnets. They draw people to them and their cause by their work ethic, sincerity, and passion. Not their hype.

5. Think Small, Not Tall

When I stepped down from the platform after delivering a speech, a university student approached me. He introduced himself and enthusiastically announced, "I'm going to feed millions of people someday. I'm going to build a major organization that will change the world."

I replied, "That's a great vision, but are you feeding anyone now?"

He was noticeably deflated by my question. "Right now I'm focused on my schoolwork."

I nodded, saying, "I understand—but you might try helping someone now to see if it's something you really want to give your life to."

Quite frankly, I saw a lot of myself in that student. I couldn't help but reflect on my conversation with Mother Teresa when she challenged me to do something. Hopefully he took my advice and is a revolutionary fighting for the poor and suffering today. If so, I'm sure he discovered that disruptive compassion is less about the limelight and more about the spotlight we place on the needs of people right in front of us.

Author John Brubaker said, "You need to ditch your big

goals and focus on achieving small daily wins. A 'goal' is too abstract and far reaching and as a result it becomes elusive."[7]

6. Find Early Wins

Although they can carry a movement only so far, early wins are important to momentum. Entrepreneur Gil Penchina said, "Momentum begets momentum, and the best way to start is to start."[8] Author Adam Braun said, "For any movement to gain momentum, it must start with a small action. This action becomes multiplied by the masses, and is made tangible when leadership changes course due to the weight of the movement's voice."[9]

IBM executive Sue Hed said early wins build team certainty: "Early wins are all about credibility and confidence. People have more faith in people who have delivered. You want your boss to have confidence in you. You want team members to have confidence in you, in themselves, and in the plan for change that has emerged. Early wins fuel that confidence."[10]

When Jesus entered public service at age thirty, he disrupted the culture with acts of compassion. Through his words and deeds, he created an early buzz. His first public miracle was turning water into wine at a wedding feast. He fed five thousand people at one time, healed the blind, and raised the dead. He criticized tyrants and exalted the oppressed. In a short time, without the help of social media, he seized the public's attention and created a wave of momentum that has lasted two thousand years.

Jesus wasn't like some rock stars who make a splash with a hit song and then disappear. He experienced early wins and remained in the headlines until his death three and a half years later. From the outset, here's how he brought attention to his cause:

- He attracted followers who advanced his message.
- He delivered a message people could personalize.
- He articulated a vision and gave people hope that tomorrow could be better than today.
- He was passionate and believable.
- He demonstrated compassion by showing genuine kindness to the unloved.
- He performed miracles that people are still talking about today.

7. Don't Be a Ball Hog

The one and only fight I had in high school took place after a basketball game. That day, everything I put up went in. I must have shot thirty times. (Kevin Durant doesn't shoot thirty times.) Behind-the-back passes, twenty-five-footers, fall-away jumpers. I couldn't miss. My teammates pretty much just fed me the ball and watched. But I knew I crossed a line when I mockingly dribbled the ball through the opposing center's legs.

Later, he came looking for me in the locker room. "You think you're good, don't you?" I pulled my polo over my head without a response. "You're a [expletive]!" he yelled. Teammates gathered around, but no one came to my defense. He threw a punch that glanced off my jaw.

"What's your problem?" I sneered.

"You're my problem," he said, winding up and connecting with my cheekbone.

That one got my attention. I confess, I didn't really want to fight. He was six inches taller and fifty pounds heavier. I kept hoping someone would break up the fight before he broke my nose. But when he loaded up for a third punch, instinct took over. I lowered my head and drove it into his stomach and pinned him to the ground. The guys cheered as we wrestled for an advantage.

Just in time, one of the coaches grabbed a wad of my shirt and hoisted me to my feet. "That's enough—both of you," he shouted.

The other guy stormed away, yelling, "This isn't done, Donaldson."

It *was* done. He never bothered me again. Nor did I attempt to dribble through another opponent's legs. That experience reminded me that ball hogs are typically on their own when times get tough. They're performers rather than leaders. True revolutionaries are like point guards in basketball; they get others involved by sharing the ball. They understand that in humanitarian work there are no MVP trophies—just team awards. Revolutionaries without a team or network are considered trash talkers. They talk big but seldom get anything done.

George Bradt said, "Individual wins, either external or internal, can be counterproductive if a leader hasn't yet gained the support of his or her team. . . . Team wins beat individual wins because teams beat individuals. Individual wins by leaders . . . can be counterproductive because they can make other team members feel inadequate or threatened."[11]

Ask yourself three questions: Are you experiencing more individual or team-oriented wins? Do you enjoy sharing the credit? And is there something you can do to invest in a team victory?

8. Invite Others to Join the Cause

Momentum builds when multiple voices, from different sectors of influence, take up your cause. Late night host Stephen Colbert encouraged viewers to donate after Typhoon Haiyan hit the Philippines. When he heard that China pledged a meager $100,000 for relief, Colbert made it his mission to inspire his fans, known as Colbert Nation, to "outgive China." He challenged viewers to donate to Convoy of Hope and raised more than $350,000, which provided one million meals, water filters, hygiene kits, building materials, and more.

YouTubers and Convoy of Hope friends Benji and Judy Travis raised more than $1.3 million to feed hungry children throughout the world by hosting an annual twenty-four-hour live broadcast where they rallied their fans to dance for donations.

In 2017, Grammy Award–winning recording artist Natalie Grant watched the devastation caused by Hurricane Harvey on television. She knew she had to do something to help survivors. She began calling friends in the music business—singers like *American Idol* finalist Danny Gokey. A few days later, they produced an online fundraising concert, and viewers responded by donating $260,000 to Convoy of Hope.

Two weeks later, K-LOVE and Air1 organized a benefit concert in Dallas for Convoy of Hope's hurricane relief efforts. Thousands came to see MercyMe, TobyMac, Casting Crowns, For King & Country, Natalie Grant, and others. Some of the performers even left their tours and drove through the night to lend their support to the cause. And that evening, more than $500,000 was raised. In total, K-Love and Air1 raised $2 million for hurricane relief.

As this kind of revolutionary, you don't have a monopoly on your cause. Many share your passion and commitment. The greatest movements experience momentum because they invite others to join them in their mission or they team up with others who are on the same mission. Harness the power of collaboration.

9. Don't Rest on Your Achievements

Film director Ron Howard said, "If you're not out there taking some risks, if you're just coasting along with your wins, then you're not really trying."[12]

Yesterday's achievements are great, but they won't accomplish tomorrow's mission. Glancing back at how far you've traveled can provide courage and encouragement to press on. But it's more important to keep your focus on the goal in front of you and to ask, "What's next?" The need before you is so great, it cannot afford for you to be infatuated with past achievements. There's simply too much that still needs to be done. When revolutionaries reach one summit, they're already looking to climb the next peak.

10. Remember Your Ideals

Do you remember the first time you said, "I want my life to count—I want to do something good in the world"? Hopefully you still feel that way, because that inner drive is vital to your mission. Pure motives and profound principles will carry you far. Regardless of where your journey takes you, hold on to the ideals that have made you who you are.

For revolutionaries, success is not based on bank accounts, press clippings, or prestigious awards. It's measured by the positive change that takes place in the lives of the people you serve. The recipients of disruptive compassion are the true picture of your movement's momentum.

CHAPTER 9

ELIMINATE
DISTRACTIONS

*The successful warrior is the average man, with
laser-like focus.*

—Bruce Lee

The instant my head collided with the escalator step, I
feared that was it—that was how my life would end.
My last breath would be taken in a Japanese train station.
Bleeding and unconscious, I rode to the top of the escalator
on my back, feet first, like a middle-aged mannequin on
a factory conveyor belt. This was not how I'd planned on
the day going down. I was riding to the second floor when
an inebriated passenger fell, colliding with pedestrian after
pedestrian on the way down. Of course, believing I was the
Hulk, I tried to catch him. But the bodies continued to fall
like dominoes, including mine. The next thing I remember
was paramedics hoisting me onto a gurney into an ambulance
and rushing me to a Japanese hospital.

We had flown to Tokyo to rendezvous with Convoy of Hope disaster relief teams. They had established distribution centers near the radiation zone following the 2011 earthquake and tsunami. For a few surreal hours, I wondered if I'd ever see those sites or make it home. But two days and one concussion later, I boarded a bullet train to survey the region.

Wearing radiation detection devices, we drove in the direction of a damaged nuclear reactor. Like a scene from a Duane Johnson action movie, men in white hazmat suits could be seen measuring radiation levels on street corners. We walked into a refugee center, where our workers were providing food, water, and supplies to families. People were sleeping on cardboard and washing clothes by hand. Toothbrushes, soap, and toilet paper were the hottest commodities. The volunteer workforce consisted of churches and pastors who refused to retreat. Instead, they distributed emergency supplies right alongside us.

Convoy of Hope has earned a reputation as a first responder when hurricanes, tornadoes, volcanoes, floods, and earthquakes hit, but that doesn't mean there aren't unforeseen challenges. The threat of radiation poisoning, for example, forced us to take extra precautions and implement new strategies. Based on government briefings, we established points of distribution in a safe zone. In the months that followed, thousands of citizens were served without a single worker being harmed.

Every mission presents its own share of challenges. Obstacles are expected in the context of humanitarian relief: supplies arrive late, transportation is nearly impossible, governments are unprepared or unresponsive. You don't want to create more obstacles by tolerating unnecessary distractions. The simplest distraction can take away your focus, render you ineffective, and lead to catastrophic mistakes.

Ask a group of students what distracts them from studying, and their list will include everything from phones to computers, friends, and physical needs. No surprises there. But distractions take on many forms:

- Fearing things you can't control
- Inviting too many opinions
- Worrying about others' reactions
- Having too many options
- Saying yes too often
- Trying to fix other people's mistakes
- Reliving the past

Distractions in the modern world are more common than you might think. The TED-Ed short "Distracted Minds" noted,

Our brain is not wired to pay attention to more than one complex task at a time. What we're actually doing when we think we are multitasking is quickly shifting our focus from one activity to another. So while our mind is engaged in applying makeup, arguing with a backseat driver, fumbling for a water bottle, or a conversation, it's blind to the road. In fact, drivers are four times more likely to crash while talking on the phone. And 23 times more likely while texting. Driving can feel uneventful, but it really takes our full attention to keep the car on the road. We're surrounded by distractions that can hijack our focus. Whether we let them is up to us.[1]

Revolutionaries will not accomplish their mission without focus, resilience, and discipline. "One way to boost our will power and focus," said Daniel Goleman, author and science journalist, "is to manage our distractions instead of letting them manage us."[2] As with many aspects of life, this is easier said than done. The Bible says, "Let your eyes look straight ahead; fix your gaze directly before you. Give careful thought to the paths for your feet and be steadfast in all your ways" (Prov. 4:25–26).

Some revolutionaries cave in to the rigors of daily life. But lack of passion and adversity are not to blame. It's often a preoccupation with things that are deemed urgent or trivial. Whether you're responding to emails, solving other people's problems, or confronting a pile of responsibility, remaining focused is among the greatest challenges you'll face. How do you channel your attention and energy when the game is on TV, friends live at your house, and you're working two jobs? Never before has your mission had to compete with so much distraction. Yet the noise cannot be allowed to choke out disruptive compassion. No battle can be won and no enemy defeated when you retreat to the mundane. No disease can be cured, no nation can be fed, no conflict can be healed, unless people like you remain focused on your mission.

For years, I was distracted by the pain of my past. Rather than setting my sights on future opportunities, I was paralyzed by the tragedy of my childhood. I couldn't embrace a vision because I was bound by flashbacks of empty cupboards and empty pockets. I knew the shame of poverty. My father, a pastor of a small church, didn't earn enough to rent a house. So we lived in the church. To save face, I hopped off my school bus a block away and walked home. I learned at an early age that I was different from my friends. They played golf after school; I went to work. They wore name brands; I relied on hand-me-downs. My life was a daily test to avoid ridicule and control my resentment toward an unfair world.

My past was a distraction because it caused me to feel inferior and incapable of accomplishing anything significant. I didn't see myself as someone who had the right education, opportunity, or background to really do something that mattered in the world. People didn't expect much from me, and I didn't have the confidence to expect much from myself. It was only when I accepted my past—and began to view my hardships differently—that I was able to break free from the chains of that distraction. Eventually my childhood circumstances became the fuel to do something good in the world so other kids didn't have to suffer.

HOW TO PREVAIL OVER DISTRACTIONS

Christopher Columbus said, "By prevailing over all obstacles and distractions, one may unfailingly arrive at his chosen goal or destination."[3] That sounds well and good, but how do you actually prevail over distractions when your typical day consists of a drive-thru for breakfast on the way to a desk job or a week of classes? What does it look like to prevail over distractions in the real world? Here are a few practical steps you can take to begin answering that question.

1. Prioritize Your Life

Revolutionaries ask themselves, "What's the most important thing for me to be doing right now? And what's taking me away from doing the most important thing?" Answering those two questions will help you eliminate distractions and put first things first.

Apple CEO Tim Cook said, "We are the most focused company that I know of. . . . We keep the amount of things we focus on very small in number so that we can put enormous energy behind the ones we do choose."[4] Apple cofounder Steve Jobs similarly advocated for focus: "That's been one of my mantras—focus and simplicity. Simple can be harder than complex: You have to work hard to get your thinking clean to make it simple. But it's worth it in the end because once you get there, you can move mountains. I'm as proud of what we don't do as I am of what we do."[5]

2. Simplify, Simplify, Simplify

Do you ever wonder why life seems to be so cluttered and complicated, both internally and externally? Sometimes the answer is because that's the way we want it. Many blame distractions on technology and entertainment choices. But according to author Kyle Cease, distractions are often a defensive mechanism: "Distractions are by-products of a problem. Something outside of you is pulling you away from yourself or a goal. But the distraction is actually on the inside, and what's going on outside matches what's going on inside."[6] He said we invite distractions to handle three internal struggles: fear, insecurity, and the need for control.

Perhaps the first step to simplifying your life is figuring out why you haven't done so already. Is the status quo of chaos just comfortable enough to keep you there? If you're juggling seven balls, is getting rid of a few unimaginable? If so, then you may be more married to your lifestyle than you realize.

Someone said, "The more you own, the more you have to worry about." That doesn't mean you sell your motor home because you don't want to be distracted by maintenance and repair issues. Or you sell your house because you don't want to mow the lawn. It means some possessions or relationships require a disproportionate amount of time and energy. In other words, they own you. To free up time, mental space, and resources, you may have to do some dumping, cutting, or letting go to create margin.

Rapper Kanye West said, "Distraction is the enemy of vision. Sometimes you have to get rid of everything."[7] Television producer and talent judge Simon Cowell said, "I hate belongings. I hate clutter. It really bothers me because I can't think properly. If you've got distractions in front of you, your mind goes nuts."[8]

A friend invited me for coffee one afternoon. He confided that he and his wife felt led to donate their car to Convoy of Hope. And it wasn't just any car. It was a 2006 Ford GT, valued at over $275,000. He had worked hard to acquire it, and now he was prepared to give it away. I asked, "Are you sure you want to do this? I know you love that car." With measured words, he replied, "It's what we're supposed to do. We believe God wants us to do this. When you auction it off, the money can be better used to feed more hungry children."

My eyes filled with tears as I considered their tangible kindness and generosity. In response, I made a commitment of my own: "I promise we'll use the money wisely."

He shook his head, saying, "I know that, but it's one less thing for me to think about and it's going to a good cause."

I pondered that conversation for weeks. Driven by their faith, they were giving the car away to help others. But it was more than that. They wanted to accomplish greater things in life, and they felt that keeping the car was unnecessary and could actually get in their way.

3. Relocate
Sometimes you have to leave where you are to get to where you want to go. That may be a night alone, a weekend

retreat, a two-week vacation, or even a complete relocation to another city. This isn't a twenty-first-century phenomenon, either. Take Jesus. He didn't have to deal with emails or texts, but the demands for his time and attention were relentless. He was surrounded by people with their own needs, not to mention the scheming elitists who were threatened by his growing popularity and determined to derail his mission. The Bible specifically records several occasions when he found a quiet place to rest, pray, and gain perspective. (See Mark 1:35.) He recognized the value—the necessity—of relocation when distractions mounted. He wasn't escaping; he was maneuvering for the sake of the mission.

4. Manage Your Schedule

Henry David Thoreau said, "It is not enough to be busy; so are the ants. The question is: What are we busy about?"[9] Motivational speaker Zig Ziglar said, "Lack of direction, not lack of time, is the problem. We all have twenty-four-hour days."[10]

Take an honest look at your calendar. How are you spending the majority of your discretionary time? Do you even know, or does it seem to just vanish? What's important and what's a distraction? Your mind probably just jumped to the fun things that consume your time. Who said fun is a distraction? Fun is as important to your health as a balanced diet. Playing golf, watching movies, gardening, and reading are essential *if* they put your mind at rest and help you rejuvenate.

I once interviewed media mogul Ted Turner. I asked, "What's the key to your success?" I expected some profound formula or philosophy. He replied simply, "Leisure time."

Who is really governing your schedule? Are your days filled with obligations placed on you by others? Do you have a hard time saying, "No, I can't do that"? If you are enslaved by the demands of others, you won't have the energy or the time to fulfill your mission. You have to learn to tactfully say no so you can say yes to your cause. Sometimes that means saying no to good (even great) opportunities, recognizing that they still compromise the mission or would require sacrificing your margin. It's easy to say no to the wrong things; it's the right things that are the hardest to turn down.

Here are some practical tips for managing your schedule:

- Turn off smart phone and desktop notifications.
- Set aside blocks of time for certain activities: email, phone calls, social media, entertainment, exercise, reading, prayer, chores, and more.
- Keep a physical or digital calendar and make it work for you.
- Follow a morning routine with only slight variations on the weekends.
- Limit caffeine intake and late-night action movies to ensure you get plenty of sleep.
- Schedule vacations that are invigorating and restful.
- Program disruptive compassion activities into your schedule: volunteering at a local church or youth center, befriending the elderly, or fixing a neighbor's bicycle, for example.

5. Give a Pep Talk

Jack Canfield, the originator of the book series Chicken Soup for the Soul, said, "Successful people maintain a positive focus in life no matter what is going on around them. They stay focused on their past successes, rather than their past failures."[11]

Your mission is doomed if you assume defeat. Nothing

good comes from negativity—it's a distraction. It's a sword that will cut you as you try to wield it. Everyone has negative thoughts, so what do we do with them? The prescription is straightforward: "Take captive" negative thoughts. (See 2 Cor. 10:5.) When negative thoughts introduce themselves, you can choose your response. You can replay those thoughts over and over until they're exaggerated. Or you can set them aside, find a mirror, and give yourself a pep talk. Call yourself out. Remind yourself of the mission and its importance. Speak truth in the face of lies: You are capable and have reason to be confident. You can make a difference. There's no reason to give up now. It may feel like the world is against you, but God and a lot of people are for you.

Excuses are often distractions too. Masquerading as "reasonable justification," they keep you from practicing disruptive compassion. For example, we see a person in need and talk ourselves out of responding: "It's not safe. They'll expect me to help every time. I don't have enough time or money. They don't like me anyway." The list of excuses is endless, and the consequences of inaction can be severe.

I witnessed this firsthand in East Africa.

After missing three rainy seasons, the region was on the verge of famine. Millions were at risk of starvation. The drought-stricken area extended to Tanzania, Somalia, Sudan, Uganda, Ethiopia, and Kenya. An estimated 70 percent of the cattle and 50 percent of the camels, goats, and sheep had died. Meanwhile, governments around the world were slow to respond and news coverage was limited.

Missionaries Mike McClaflin and Greg Beggs formulated a plan to rescue a village in northern Kenya. Convoy of Hope would provide food and supplies, and Worldserve and Africa Oasis Project would drill a well.

Our twelve-passenger plane landed on a remote landing strip. Immediately I noticed that creek beds, bushes, and animals had been virtually swallowed by sand. A large pond now resembled a rock quarry. Trees slumped like weary soldiers after a battle. There was no sign of life.

Land Rovers with armed soldiers met the plane to transport us to the village. They would also escort a large truck filled with emergency food. Bandits were known to hijack supply trucks at gunpoint on this long, dusty road.

"These people have lost everything," our African guide said as our Land Rover streaked toward the village. "Many have died—poisoned by water infected with typhoid."

My eyes fell upon the skeletal remains of animals and the vultures feasting on them. Nearby an elderly man with a gaunt face and lifeless eyes squatted alongside the road. I knew we couldn't stop so I didn't ask, but I knew he was only hanging on.

A few miles down the road, a flat tire brought the convoy to a halt. We hopped out to stretch our legs. Like a mirage, a caravan of families and camels laden with empty water receptacles appeared in the distance and slowly approached us. Through an interpreter, a young man told me they had traveled three days without locating water and their food supply was running out. When we gave them water, they bowed gratefully, as if they'd been given a new lease on life.

An hour later, we arrived at the village to a hero's welcome. Men and children danced in celebration. Women sang. Two men blew horns.

After greeting us on behalf of the village, the chief ordered his men to unload the truck. The crowd surrounded the vehicle, and with each box of food, they erupted into louder and louder cheers. This was their miracle, the day they had dreamed of for months. With the food—and promise of more food—and a new well, they knew they'd survive at least another season.

Hundreds of villagers survived the famine in large part because missionaries and relief workers refused to be deterred. They could have made excuses and allowed distractions to blockade the relief effort. They could have fixed their eyes on the bandits, logistics, expense, and health risks. Instead, they focused on what they could do and the lives that would be lost if they didn't respond.

Returning to the plane, I gave my friend a pat on the back. "Job well done, Mike."

"Team effort," he replied flatly.

Rather than revel in victory, the former logistics officer in Vietnam only wanted to discuss the next shipment of food and the next well to be drilled. No distractions. No excuses. As far as he was concerned, our job wasn't done.

If you've ever used a malfunctioning GPS device, sometimes you don't know there's a problem until you arrive at the wrong destination. Distractions are a lot like that—they send you in the opposite direction and prevent you from achieving your mission. Eliminating distractions will bring focus to your mission and, as you'll read in the next chapter, increase your opportunities for taking risks.

CHAPTER 10

TAKE RISKS

If it wasn't hard, everyone would do it. It's the hard that makes it great.

—Tom Hanks

Inside Convoy of Hope's state-of-the-art war room, Kirk Noonan and I watched video reports of the devastation in Indonesia, Sri Lanka, and Thailand. A massive tsunami had just flattened villages and killed more than 100,000 people. Before our eyes ran footage of orphaned children wandering aimlessly and families pleading to be rescued. This wasn't the first time I'd witnessed the aftermath of a disaster—it wasn't even the second or third—but that didn't matter. I was at a loss for words.

Kirk wasted no time. "I need to be on the next flight to Indonesia."

"It's dangerous," I said.

"We gotta go," he said.

I knew he was right. But I never liked the idea of sending team members into harm's way. After a few seconds, I nodded. "Okay. You head to Indonesia. I'll take a team to Sri Lanka."

Thirty-six hours later, Kirk stood in an area of Indonesia controlled by extremists. The stench of death was suffocating, but it wasn't the smell that nearly knocked Kirk to his knees. It was the sight of lifeless children. Bodies were stacked alongside the roads. He had just entered what felt like an alternate reality.

While interviewing a survivor, he noticed a group of men encircling him. Emotions always run high following a disaster, so Kirk told himself to remain calm as he scanned the area for the other members of his media team. They were nowhere to be found. Sensing danger, he turned to leave. It was too late. Without warning, one man shoved the survivor aside and stood in Kirk's way.

"Where are you from?" the man demanded.

"The United States," Kirk replied.

Pointing his finger, the man snapped, "Then you hate us."

Stepping back, Kirk said, "If I hated you or your people, why would I leave my family and travel halfway around the world to a disaster zone to help you? I don't hate anyone."

The man shoved his finger in Kirk's chest. "We don't want your help," he spat. "All Americans hate us!"

"That's not true," Kirk countered. "I work for Convoy of Hope. We respond to disasters all over the world. We're here to help anyone who needs it—"

"We don't want your help!"

The group pressed in on Kirk from all sides, shouting and cursing at him.

God, what should I do? Kirk prayed silently.

What happened next didn't make sense even to Kirk, but may have been just the thing that saved his life. He started speaking in broken Spanish. The men looked at one another, confused. Seizing the moment, Kirk spun and pushed his way through the throng of angry men and onlookers. He hustled to the end of the road where the van he had hired pulled up just as the throng was closing in on him again.

"Who were those guys?" Kirk asked as they drove away.

The van driver shook his head. "They are from a terrorist group and they want to kill you."

When you're committed to disruptive compassion, you may find yourself in tough places. Sure, probably not a disaster zone occupied by extremists. But you may feel overmatched because the unknowns outnumber the knowns. But changing the world is impossible if everyone plays it safe. How will disaster survivors, for example, be rescued if no one risks going to dark places? How will injustice end if no one stands up and says, "Enough"?

Through the efforts of Convoy of Hope's disaster relief team, thousands of tsunami survivors received food, water, emergency supplies, and shelter. But it all began with revolutionaries who said, "I'll go," and many, many others who said, "I'll give."

Disruptive compassion is a lot like skydiving. Your palms are sweating and you feel safer in your seatbelt. You scream to yourself, *This is insane—I can't do this!* But once you've mustered the courage to jump, initial terror gives way to exhilaration. And when your feet finally hit the ground, you tell yourself, *I want to do that again!* Likewise, it gets easier each time you step out of your comfort zone and help someone in need. Before long you'll discover that disruptive compassion is no longer an occasional good deed—it's become a lifestyle.

Revolutionaries of this kind are risk-takers, but they aren't necessarily daredevils. They don't jump out of airplanes without parachutes or soar over buses on motorcycles. They acknowledge danger and weigh potential reward. They know the difference between recklessness and reasonable risk. They ask themselves, "What's the worst that can happen if I fail? Will failure impact more than just me? What is the likelihood that I will fail?" General George Patton said, "Take calculated risks—that is quite different from being rash."[1]

You're probably asking, "What exactly does a risk look like?" It's different for everyone, but risks have this in common: They have the potential for failure. The outcome isn't guaranteed. The results are up in the air. But compassion revolutionaries are compelled to try because their desire for success is stronger than their fear of failure. Ralph Waldo Emerson said, "Do not be too timid and squeamish about your actions. All life is an experiment. The more experiments you make the better."[2]

If you think risk is avoidable, you're wrong. Life is, as one writer put it, "a series of calculated risks—nothing more. Everything that you decide to do has a margin of risk. No outcome is ever 100 percent certain and, therefore, any attempt at anything has a chance of complete failure. We risk everything, every day of our lives without knowing it."[3]

Take a look at this list from author Paul Hudson and consider the risks you've already taken. Then think about the ones you still want to take:

- Risk being rejected by a love interest.
- Risk not getting the dream job.
- Risk a financial investment not paying off.
- Risk starting a family.
- Risk moving away from home.
- Risk saying I love you.

- Risk saying I'm sorry.
- Risk saying no to an opportunity for something greater.
- Risk starting when you don't feel fully prepared.
- Risk not having what it takes.
- Risk saying "I don't know."
- Risk being honest.[4]

Your life is a reflection of the risks you've taken. For example, years ago you may have introduced yourself to someone you found attractive. You took the risk, even though you knew rejection was a possibility. Two years later, you walked the aisle to marry him or her. Or perhaps you accepted a job with a company right out of college. You were so nervous, you wanted to call in sick on day one. You felt totally unprepared for that job, but somehow you mustered the courage to try. Five years have now passed and you couldn't imagine working anywhere else. Or perhaps you took $5,000 and purchased stock in a burgeoning company. Six months later, you doubled your money. Romance, career, investments—much of what you value in life (even those things not on the list) require a risk.

Revolutionaries take risks even when they're afraid because they're more fearful of the consequences of not taking them. Facebook CEO Mark Zuckerberg said, "The biggest risk is not taking any risk. . . . In a world that's changing really quickly, the only strategy that is guaranteed to fail is not taking risks."[5] And First Lady Eleanor Roosevelt said, "Do one thing every day that scares you."[6] Michael Jordan said, "I can accept failure. Everybody fails at something. But I can't accept not trying. Fear is an illusion."[7]

Sometimes disruptive compassion won't make any sense,

and it will force you to move from your comfort zone. But for revolutionaries, that's exactly why following disruptive compassion is such an adventure. It requires risk. It's seeing needs and opportunities and being compelled to respond. At first, you feel underprepared and under-resourced. Like me, you may ask yourself, *What am I doing here? What's gotten into me? There are thousands of people better equipped to meet this need than me.* Then reality hits you in the face and you hear a voice say, *But those thousands of people aren't here—you are.*

For you, compassion-related risks may involve helping someone you don't know, going places you'd prefer not to be, or speaking up when no one else will. But remember, each day is not a performance to be graded. It's part of a much greater adventure in doing your part to change the world. There's room for trying and failing. No one is looking over your shoulder critiquing your words or evaluating your actions. And even if someone is doing that, a single opinion or judgment is not your rubric. So what if you say or do the wrong thing? So what if, in hindsight, you wish you had done something differently? Just say or do something different next time. The only real failure is allowing fear to keep you from doing something that needs to be done. Or as the apostle Paul said, "Watch your step. Use your head. Make the most of every chance you get. These are desperate times!" (Eph. 5:15–16 MSG).

T. S. Eliot said, "Only those who will risk going too far can possibly find out how far it is possible to go."[8] And it was Mark Twain who said, "Twenty years from now you will be more disappointed by the things you didn't do than by the ones you did. So throw off the bowlines, sail away from the safe harbor, catch the trade winds in your sails. Explore. Dream. Discover."[9]

It's impossible to talk about risk without talking about fear, because fear is at the root of our aversion to risk. Not all fear is bad, but it is often misplaced. As one author noted, we should "fear regret more than failure—history has shown that we fail far more from timidity than we do from over daring. . . . When weighing . . . whether to take an action that could leave us vulnerable to failing or some other form of loss (of reputation, money, social standing, pride, etc.), we have an innate tendency to misjudge . . . elements in assessing risk."[10]

Whether you consider yourself a relatively brave or fearful person—you're human. You're going to have a tendency to play it safe and avoid risk in certain areas of your life. But you can determine where to go from there by asking these questions:

- What's something I have avoided in the last six months because of fear?
- What would I do in life if fear wasn't a factor?
- What are the consequences of letting fear hold me back in different areas of my life?
- Are any of those consequences enough to make me want to reconsider holding back?
- Are there any fears that I might be overestimating?
- Are there any risks I regret not taking?
- What could I do differently to overcome obstacles and take more risks?

I was justifiably nervous to ride shotgun on the midnight shift with a Miami police officer. Perhaps I had a premonition of what was to come. It was shortly after 1:30 a.m. when a stolen car barrelled into a jewelry store—what the officer called a "smash and grab." Seconds later, four thieves burst out carrying bags of stolen property. Before I knew what was happening, the officer was running after the perpetrators and so was I. Doing my best to keep pace, we chased the culprits across a dark field and down an empty street. Already out of breath, I felt my throat catch when I saw the officer place his hand on his gun. All I had was a flashlight. *Am I out of my mind? What happens if we catch them? What if they have guns? This is beyond risk-taking—this is craziness.* Unfortunately for the officer (but luckily for me), we heard the squealing tires of a getaway car and gave up the chase.

Later that night, I met a sixteen-year-old gangbanger named David who admitted he'd been involved in smash and grabs and drive-by shootings. He stood with his tatted shoulders back, chest out, spine sentry-straight, and chin raised. He agreed to talk to me off the record.

"If you snitch me, I'm coming at you," he said.

I nodded. "No problem—I won't use names." I couldn't help but wonder if it was safe talking to him in an open diner.

"I may die before I'm twenty, but, bro, I'm livin' the way I want to live," he said. "I make lots of money watchin' our girls and doing tats—I can do that as long as I want—and no one's going to [expletive] with me."

He fielded all my questions, though glancing at his watch every few minutes.

"You in a hurry?" I asked.

"Got someplace to be—what else you wanna know?"

"You regret anything you've done?"

He glared at me as if contemplating his answer.

"Yeah. My mom—she worries about me."

I paused for him to elaborate. Instead, he rose to leave. "Next time you're in town, look me up and I'll give you a free tat," he said over his shoulder.

Again my inner dialogue swirled. *What am I doing here? Is writing a magazine article or book really worth putting my life on the line? These are bad dudes. There's nothing I can do to change them because they really don't want to change.*

I stepped out of the diner into a downpour, so I quickly ducked under an awning with other pedestrians. Standing next to me was a twentysomething with spiked white hair and painted nails. As we chatted, I noticed his hands were shaking. "You cold?" I asked.

"I'm sick," he replied. After a long pause, he added, "AIDS, bro."

His story was tragic. There was no other word for it. And as I listened to him, something broke inside me. I walked to an empty street corner and looked to the heavens. "God! What do you expect from me? Don't you know? People are dying! What can we do? What am I supposed to do?" Like a film noir scene, rain continued to fall as shadows danced around me. It was a picture of what was happening on the inside. Unfortunately, no answers fell with the drops. Yet even in this moment—one of my bleakest, most desperate, most throw-up-my-hands-and-swear-at-the-world moments—I was beginning to see that changing the world was impossible unless I was willing to take extraordinary risks. I had to be willing to go to forgotten places and engage with desperate people. Their lives depended on it and so did mine. That short time in Miami is what it took to show me that a life without risk is a life without influence, and a life without influence leads to a world without hope.[11]

Convoy of Hope had just celebrated its two-year

anniversary when I was invited to speak at a business luncheon. Afterward, a man pushed a business card into my hand as he introduced himself. "Hi, my name is David Cribbs," he said. "Please come and see me sometime."

Four weeks passed before I entered David's office. He didn't waste any time. "My family wants to buy Convoy of Hope a tractor trailer. I'll provide you with a driver and all the fuel and maintenance for a year. After that it's your responsibility. How does that sound?"

I tried to act like this wasn't our first big breakthrough, but in reality that's *exactly* what it was. "That would be incredible," I replied, tears threatening my eyes. At the time, we were borrowing a box truck and leasing a small warehouse. David had no idea that weeks earlier I had written the following note and placed it in my desk: *If we're going to expand the reach of Convoy of Hope, this is what we need: trucks, warehouses, food, and funding.*

Several months later, we held a dedication celebration for our first tractor trailer. During the ceremony, my friend Doug Clay, the national youth director for the Assemblies of God, asked, "How many of these trucks do you need?"

I thought for a moment, not wanting to aim too high or too low. I replied, "Someday we'd like to have ten."

He paused for a moment and said, "I think we can do that." That's how Convoy of Hope's fleet of tractor trailers became a reality. It began with people who were willing to take a risk on an organization that was far from a sure thing.

These miracles led to our next challenge. After all, it didn't make sense to own a fleet of tractor trailers without a warehouse. Initially, we figured we could get by with a ten-thousand-square-foot facility. We had begun searching for leasing options when a member of our team received a phone call from a business owner. He said he owned "the ideal warehouse for Convoy of Hope." It was 300,000 square feet, with forty-one loading docks and had just hit the market for $8 million. I phoned David Cribbs and a new friend from Pennsylvania, Gerry Hindy, and asked if they would tour the building with me. Gerry owned numerous businesses, and he and David specialized in real estate negotiations. After touring the facility and studying our financials, Gerry and David shook their heads. Realistically, they knew the building was well out of our reach. It would require taking a major risk that could cripple the organization. The only way we could qualify for a mortgage was if the price was greatly reduced, we received a large donation, and tenants were in place to lease portions of the building. That was all—three tiny prerequisites.

"Are you sure you want to move forward?" Gerry asked.

I nodded. "I think we're supposed to have the building."

David said, "Then let's talk to the owner and see what he'll do."

"I agree," Gerry said.

That moment of arguably illogical faith, courage, and risk-taking opened the door to the impossible. Within weeks, all three of our requirements were met, and we took possession of the massive facility that would catapult Convoy of Hope in the years to come.

With a fleet of trucks and a huge warehouse, the organization began expanding its vision. We began testing community outreaches across the nation. We knew it was a risk to host five to ten thousand guests at a city park, but as Pablo Picasso said, "I am always doing that which I cannot do, in order that I may learn how to do it."[12] With each outreach, we learned how to make the events safer and more effective. We learned how to provide adequate security, fencing, tents, toilets, supplies, and emergency medical care. And we learned how to train volunteers and bring churches, civic organizations, businesses, and government agencies together.

But one outreach in Minneapolis presented an unusual set of problems. More than three thousand guests were waiting in line when the food delivery truck rolled up to the outreach site at 7:30 a.m. Another organization had pledged to provide the food if Convoy of Hope oversaw the logistics. But when we opened the back of the truck, the entire team let out an audible gasp. Inside were two pallets of carrots and onions and a few boxes of baby food. In addition there were some large, unlabeled "mystery" cans. Hardly an appetizing meal. Even if given with the best of intentions, this product simply couldn't be distributed to the thousands of guests who had arrived expecting nutritious groceries for themselves and their families. Distributing these pallets would completely contradict Convoy's "guest of honor" principle, which says every person at an outreach should be honored like royalty. No one should be treated as a charity case. They deserved the best we could offer.

Thinking quickly, I hopped in a car and raced to a local supermarket. I introduced myself to the manager and held up my personal credit card. "What can I buy for $15,000?" I asked. He led me back to his storeroom and said, "Happy shopping."

We learned about the risk and rewards of partnership that day, but the outreach was a huge success despite the less conventional road taken to get there. Lots of families received help, and we gained more knowledge in our toolbox for the future.

Later that afternoon, one of the volunteers introduced me

to a guest. He said his name was Marvin and he wanted to make a cash donation for the event.

"How much did the food cost?" he asked.

"Fifteen thousand dollars," I answered reluctantly (although I had the receipt to prove it).

"I don't have that on me," he replied, "but I have it at my house."

He motioned for me to follow him.

I hesitated. "That would be a big help, but I can't leave the outreach."

"I live a mile away—we'll be back in twenty minutes," he urged.

Still hopeful, I asked, "Any chance you could go get it and bring it back?"

"Don't have a car here," he said. "Man, I'm offering you fifteen grand."

Finally, I relented. "Okay, let's go."

Walking to my rental car, I stopped abruptly. I couldn't quite pinpoint it, but somehow I sensed I was putting myself at great risk.

"Man, I really can't leave," I said.

"I'm outta here," he said, cursing as he darted into the crowd.

I said to myself, "We could have used the money—I hope I did the right thing."

An hour later, I was still questioning my decision when I struck up a conversation with a uniformed police officer. He had come to the community event to provide added security.

"Thanks for coming and helping us out today," I said.

"My pleasure—this neighborhood really needs this," he replied.

"The medical and dental care, free shoes, groceries, and

haircuts take care of immediate needs," I explained. "But the real goal is to connect guests to job opportunities, community programs, and churches that can help them set a new direction for their lives."

"That's a great thing," he said, before shifting his focus. "I can't believe that dude's here."

"Who?" I asked.

He pointed to the same guest who had approached me earlier. "He's one of the biggest gang members in the area," he explained.

I swallowed. "Wow—that guy wanted me to go to his house so he could make a donation."

He grimaced. "I'm not sure you would've come back. He's got a rap sheet a mile long."

I was instantly glad I followed my instincts.

If you take the wrong risks, you might find yourself facing danger, financial hardship, or even personal attacks. Revolutionaries calculate risks, and when it doesn't feel right and the evidence doesn't add up, they possess the courage to retrace their steps or change course. Seriously—why risk your life for $15,000?

SIX QUESTIONS TO ASK YOURSELF

When standing at the door of risk, here are six questions to ask yourself before turning the knob.

1. Can I Handle Criticism?

In the early days of Convoy of Hope, we dealt with our share of criticism. Some condemned the full menu of services offered at our community outreaches. "That's the government's responsibility," they'd say. "These people are just freeloaders." One day, a husband and wife approached me with fire in their eyes. "Who do you think you are?" the wife demanded. "You're just making the problem worse. These people are poor because of their own mistakes. There are plenty of jobs out there, but they're not willing to work. We won't give you a dime. It's not our responsibility to pay their bills so they can sit at home and do nothing."

"You know," I countered, "what you just said is pretty hard to explain to an eight-year-old who has cavities and holes in his shoes."

"That's their parents' responsibility," the husband barked.

"Who said they have parents?" I replied.

"That's when the government steps in."

"The government doesn't have enough money or the infrastructure to fix every problem," I said. "Unless you want to give 75 percent of your income to the government."

"Your way," the wife repeated, "isn't going to fix the problem either."

"You're right, but it will fix some—and it will fix us. Every box of cereal and every pair of shoes we give away makes us more grateful for what we have. Millions of people want to escape poverty, but they don't know how. People like you and me can join them on that journey and help them find a way out."

That conversation ended quickly. *Very* quickly. Fortunately, I refrained from saying what was really on my mind: *You pompous, arrogant, ungrateful hypocrites. Go home, turn off the television talk shows, and read the Good Book—about the one who helped a stranger left for dead on the side of the road. Read about the one who decided to sacrifice it all because of his love for others. Read about what tangible kindness and generosity look like. Then maybe you'll see what you're missing in life.* Instead, I bit my tongue and said, "Thank you for your concern—pray for us."

When you decide to be a revolutionary, you invite ridicule. You become a target. Ask yourself, "Am I willing to risk ridicule and slander to make the world a better place? Will I become a revolutionary if it means taking the journey alone?"

2. Do I Need to Lead?

Leaders tend to get most of the praise and criticism. For that reason, you may want to be dubbed the leader. But following is just as important as leading. Some revolutionaries are actually born to follow other revolutionaries. Following is a calling— perhaps the most overlooked of callings. Organizations like Convoy of Hope couldn't exist without leaders and followers. Some equate following to being a hireling on minimum wage. But the follower role is actually strategic and essential to the success of any mission. It's more noble to be a great follower than a poor leader. Every follower is a leader, influencing others in some way. But take an honest look at yourself. If you're a gifted leader, lead something. Otherwise, link up with a group of people who share your passion and advance a mission together.

Derek Sivers's TED talk illustrates how following is critical to any movement. A video shows a man dancing eccentrically at an outdoor event. For a moment, he's all alone. Then another dancer joins in the fun. Sivers describes what happens next:

Now, notice that the leader embraces him as an equal. Now it's not about the leader anymore; it's about them, plural. Now, there he is calling to his friends. Now, if you notice that the first follower is actually an underestimated form of leadership in itself. It takes guts to stand out like that. The first follower is what transforms a lone nut into a leader. And here comes a second follower. Now it's not a lone nut, it's not two nuts—three is a crowd, and a crowd is news. So a movement must be public. It's important to show not just the leader, but the followers, because you find that new followers emulate the followers, not the leader. Now, here come two more people, and immediately after, three more people. Now we've got momentum. This is the tipping point. Now we've got a movement. So, notice that, as more people join in, it's less risky. So those that were sitting on the fence before now have no reason not to. They won't stand out, they won't be ridiculed, but they will be part of the in-crowd if they hurry. So, over the next minute, you'll see all of those that prefer to stick with the crowd because eventually they would be ridiculed for not joining in. And that's how you make a movement.[13]

Sivers points out the key lessons:

- Leaders relate to their first few followers as equals.
- Leadership is overly glorified.
- Movements require followers who show others how to follow.
- Some are destined to stand with someone who's trying to do something great.

3. Can I Accept Change?

Everyone wants change until it starts. For example, we want perfectly straightened teeth until the braces start to reposition our teeth. Ouch. At first, change can be appealing, until the outcomes disappoint. How many coaches of sports teams have been fired only to see their successors lose even more games? How many elected officials were voted out of office only for the electorate to be disappointed by their replacements? Sometimes change is the last thing you want. It's daunting and paralyzing when you look at the amount of work, risk, and perseverance change can require.

Guy Kawasaki served as the chief evangelist for Apple. As a student of innovation, he said change is difficult because we become married to one version of ourselves or one idea of what our lives should look like. According to Kawasaki, we need people to take risks to change the status quo in the world, but they also must be willing to change the status quo they have created (and become attached to) for themselves.[14]

In other words, don't be married to your first draft. Instead, take the risks associated with change.

4. Can I Cope with Failure?

Let's face it, some of the best acts of compassion don't produce preferred outcomes. Maybe you're unable to see how a risk you took really paid off. That's just how life is sometimes. Disruptive compassion isn't a formula. It doesn't always yield positive results. Perhaps you befriended someone who, in turn, betrayed you. Or you tried to help a youth escape drugs and he or she laughed in your face. The natural response is to throw up your hands and say, "I'm done." But that approach won't make you a revolutionary and certainly won't change the world. For revolutionaries, the goal isn't to avoid failure. The goal is to give success a chance.

5. Can I Deal with Success?

Arrogance and risk-taking often gravitate to one another. Leaders can begin to feel invincible when one gamble after another pays off. But success can lead to reckless, and sometimes catastrophic, decisions. Effective revolutionaries maintain a level of humility. They don't allow themselves to assume that past achievement guarantees future success. They know they're fallible and susceptible to errors in judgment, and the moment pride takes the driver's seat is the moment you can bet trouble is on its way.

6. What Can I Afford?

Successful businesses study the risk-return tradeoff. They determine what they can afford by creating worst-case scenarios. They want to know what failure will cost the company. Usually the higher the investment, the higher the risk and anticipated return, but also the more expensive the failure. The highest investment you can make is dedicating your life to something you believe in. Your life also presents the highest risk and the greatest potential for good.

In the years ahead, you will face challenges and receive many opportunities. As a revolutionary, you may find that your greatest struggles are not from everyday problems. Your greatest threats may be from the "wrong opportunities at the right time." Every opportunity has the power to knock you off track from your primary mission. Before you move forward, think about where that opportunity will take you. What is the risk-return tradeoff? Have you considered a worst-case scenario? Have you had sufficient time to collect intel, seek counsel, and pray? Whatever the decision, make sure you don't trade your life's mission and calling for a short-lived opportunity.

The crowd mushroomed so rapidly at the outreach in Ozd, Hungary, that we feared a riot or stampede might ensue. Ten thousand guests descended on an abandoned soccer stadium to receive a hot meal, free groceries, medical and dental care, shoes, haircuts, and more. Desperate for help, some attempted to hop the fence; others made like human battering rams to break through the gate.

"Keep the gates closed until we're all set up," Michael McNamee instructed.

"We can't wait much longer," a volunteer replied.

An arm reached through the fence and grabbed my shirt. Instinctively I pulled back—until I saw it was a small boy wanting to shake my hand. His smudged face and faded T-shirt hinted of neglect, but his smile showed hope brighter than I'd seen all day. I took his hand and smiled, regretting I couldn't hoist him over the fence to make sure his needs were met. But I knew he had to wait with everyone else.

Michael and his wife, Beryl, had led many community outreaches in Europe, but they had seldom seen such despair. Ozd was a once-thriving industrial town located near the Bükk Mountains. When the town's iron factories shut down following the Cold War, thirteen thousand workers lost their jobs, and unemployment, poverty, and crime skyrocketed. The population plummeted. Schools closed. And businesses boarded up their doors forever.

When the gates finally opened, parents ran to the groceries and children raced to the cotton candy. This would be a day of fun and relief for a community that had understandably lost almost every shred of hope.

"Thank you," a woman said, flanked by her two children. "My son has new shoes and my girl had her tooth fixed. These groceries will help us. We've been going to the forest to find mushrooms to eat."

Michael and Beryl's efforts to establish Convoy of Hope in Europe brought help to one million people in forty countries. They took a risk, and it proved to be the right opportunity at the right time.

President Jimmy Carter said, "Go out on a limb. That's where the fruit is."[15] What keeps us from taking the "highest risk" and crawling out on the limb of human need? Most of the time it's self-preservation. We've all heard stories of Good Samaritans who were burned. But the risk of practicing disruptive compassion is lower than the risk of being ticketed for jaywalking, getting sick by consuming raw fish, or getting struck by lightning (yeah, we did the math). In other words, you can afford to risk compassion by putting your labor, resources, friendship, encouragement, insight, smile, and helping hands to use. Resist the temptation to magnify the risks to the point that you play it safe, because it's not unusual for small acts of compassion to pay major dividends.

CHAPTER 11

MEASURE OUTCOMES

If you can't measure it, you can't improve it.

—Peter Drucker

For a place named Blessed of God, it wasn't living up to its name. A four-year drought in Nicaragua had cost the farmers almost everything. They'd eaten their goats and chickens and pulled their kids out of school to work in the fields. Every sunrise and sunset without rain was another reminder that their fate was sealed. The scorched ground would not produce a harvest.

But a solution was on the horizon.

Dr. Jason Streubel—"Dr. Dirt," as he is affectionately called—had come to Convoy of Hope from Washington State University. There, he had dedicated himself to learning how dirt, minerals, and manure could actually change the world. "In other words," he'd say, "I specialize in deriving information from anaerobically digested dairy manure so I can determine its ability to sequester phosphorus."

Dr. Dirt advised farmers in Nicaragua to begin growing dragon fruit, a cacti ideally suited for desert-like climates.

At first, the farmers were skeptical. They had farmed the same way for decades.

But Dr. Dirt persisted. He said, "This will work, but it will take at least two years before you see a harvest. And four years before you see a maximum harvest. You'll be able to sell them locally for $1 and sell them for $5 to exporters."

Eventually the farmers agreed and the dragon fruit project was born. Country director Pablo Gomez and Convoy of Hope's team of agronomists walked alongside the farmers every step of the way.

Seven months passed and Dr. Dirt received a phone call from Pablo. "You've got to get down here!" he exclaimed.

Dr. Dirt held his breath for bad news but instead heard something that stopped him in his tracks: "The dragon fruit is ready for harvest."

When he didn't hear a reply, Pablo assumed the reception was bad and repeated himself. "The dragon fruit is ready for harvest, Dr. Jason!"

"That *never* happens," Jason said. "It's a miracle. I need to fly down and see this for myself."

A week later, Jason and Pablo felt like they were living in a fairy tale as they inspected the fruit. Word of the miracle spread throughout the country. Government representatives and hopeful farmers began visiting the dragon-fruit fields like tourists flocking to a national monument. "Blessed of God" was finally living up to its name.

Dr. Dirt and Convoy of Hope's team of agronomists have helped more than twenty thousand farmers around the world increase their yields, often by 200 to 300 percent. Farmers in these programs save 10 percent of their seed and designate another 10 percent of their harvest to help feed children in their country through other Convoy of Hope programs.

It was simple for Dr. Dirt and Pablo to measure outcomes related to dragon fruit. The fields either produce fruit or they don't, right? But evaluating the outcomes of disruptive compassion is less straightforward.

And you may even be asking, "Why should I worry about measuring results anyway? Isn't it enough to practice disruptive compassion—to do a good deed—and carry on with my life?" Fair questions. And yes, sometimes doing a good deed and walking away are enough. But if you walk away every time and don't think twice, there's a chance your good intentions aren't any more than that—good intentions. Measuring outcomes confirms whether you're helping or hurting a situation.

I remember giving a young guy $200 to buy new clothes so he could interview for a job. He was rough around the edges and hadn't had the easiest time, so I was hoping a job could help him turn things around. Several months passed and he didn't return my calls. Naturally I was worried, so I contacted his mother. She shared the disappointing news: her son had taken the money and run away. She assured me he was okay, but I never heard from him again. I still hope and pray he pulls things together, but it was a valuable lesson for me. My good intentions had enabled this kid to make a poor decision. Although I didn't need to take responsibility for his choice, the experience reiterated the truth that good intentions don't necessarily produce good results.

The same is true in relief and development work. If we truly exist to serve the vulnerable, then they deserve our best. And we can't know if they're getting our best if we don't measure and improve our effectiveness. In their book *More*

Than Good Intentions, Dean Karlan and Jacob Appel tell us to "find individual programs that work, and support them. Find programs that don't work, and stop doing them. And observe the patterns of both to learn which conditions are conducive to success, so that our first attempts at designing solutions get better and better."[1]

This is the exact opposite of what has been dubbed "lazy thinking." In their book on global poverty, authors Abhijit V. Banerjee and Esther Duflo said, "It is possible to make the world a better place—probably not tomorrow, but in some future that is within our reach—but we cannot get there with lazy thinking."[2]

Lazy thinking is the kind that says, "I'll be nice, and if it makes a difference, great, and if not, oh well." Revolutionaries acknowledge that their responsibility is not simply to be nice and hope for the best, but rather to actually give their best and continually learn. They are active thinkers. They hold themselves accountable for more than good intentions by measuring outputs and outcomes. In disruptive compassion, outputs are the acts of kindness, and outcomes are the changes to the status quo resulting from those acts of kindness. For example, if you give someone a ride to work after his or her car breaks down, the ride given is the output and the outcome is the encouragement and friendship experienced.

PRINCIPLES FOR MEASURING OUTPUTS AND OUTCOMES

Measuring outputs and outcomes doesn't guarantee that acts of kindness will produce positive results, but it may help you make an informed decision next time around.[3] We'll talk more about the "next time around" in chapter 12, but first let's examine four principles for revolutionaries to consider when measuring outputs and outcomes.

1. Some Acts of Compassion Cannot Be Measured

As one author put it, "We may not yet have all the right tools, methods, and processes to recognize and measure outcomes, but that's no reason not to try."[4] Good metrics are behavior changing and lead to stronger outcomes.[5] But measurability is not a prerequisite to disruptive compassion.

It's obvious that evaluating the outcomes of some acts of disruptive compassion is more difficult than measuring a dragon fruit yield or a company's bottom line. Sometimes it's nearly impossible. For example, when you help a stranger at a crosswalk or lend your cell phone to a stranded motorist, you will probably never see that person again. Or when you donate to hungry children in Asia, you will likely never meet them. Or when you tutor grade schoolers, you don't know what impact that will have on their future. But here's the thing: no one ever said *every* act of compassion had to be measurable or measured. That's not practical. Revolutionaries respond to needs because it's the right thing to do, and they measure when they can. It's that simple.

2. You're Not the Judge of Lost Causes

When you're practicing disruptive compassion and outputs don't appear to produce positive outcomes, it's easy for cynicism to kick in. You tell yourself, *I'm not going to help them again because it's a waste of time, money, and energy. Besides, nothing's going to change anyway.* Unfortunately, that way of thinking sustains the status quo and doesn't help anyone. In every situation, there will be myriad factors you can't control. I couldn't control how that kid spent my $200. And yes, in the future I'd probably use a different approach, but I'm still glad I responded to the opportunity. It's important to remember you aren't responsible for every outcome, but you are responsible for every opportunity.

If you worry *too* much about accidentally helping a lost cause, you'll end up doing nothing at all. If you fear wasting kindness, you'll hold on to your resources so tightly no one will be deemed deserving. Kindness is a renewable resource. There's enough to go around. So pay attention to opportunities and anticipate the outcomes.

As revolutionaries we see things differently. Where some see insurmountable challenges, we see unprecedented opportunities. And where others see inevitable defeat, we anticipate victory. But this means we also measure return on investment differently. Today many businesses are rejecting the traditional for-profit/nonprofit dichotomy. Instead they're asking, "What is created when resources, inputs, processes or policies are combined to generate improvements in the lives of individuals or society as a whole?"[6]

What social enterprise did to the traditional bottom line, disruptive compassion does to the traditional definition of a good return on investment. Traditional thinking would say, "Don't waste your time or money by investing in people who are lost causes." Disruptive compassion says, "No one is beyond reach. There are no lost causes. But even if there are, we're not here to judge, just help." We have all seen, in big ways or small, the power of a smile, a kind word, and a helping hand. I've seen the lives of gang members, inmates, runaways, and prostitutes transformed by a kind word and a helping hand. Maybe you, too, have seen hostile neighbors and spiteful family members change because of one act of compassion.

According to the US Office of Management and Budget, the value of a human life is between seven and nine million dollars.[7] Notice this is a range, not a set figure. Apparently it's assumed some lives are "worth" more than others based on earning power, age, health, and various other factors. In contrast, the Bible and the Declaration of Independence maintain that a human life is more valuable than anything in the world. (See John 3:16; Matt. 10:29–31.) Every human life has equal value, regardless of academic achievement, wealth, or social media following. Nobel Peace Prize recipient Desmond Tutu said, "Your ordinary acts of love and hope point to the extraordinary promise that every human life is of inestimable value."[8]

Revolutionary thinking doesn't see the human race as a hierarchical organizational chart, where each member is assigned a rank. Instead, it dignifies every person as an indispensable trophy of the Creator. Revolutionaries refuse to carelessly discard people as perpetual failures. It's not their place to evaluate whether someone is worth another expenditure of kindness.

Just take a look at how Jesus saw the people he encountered. He saw potential in the poor blind man, the ostracized leper, the shunned adulteress, the tax collector, and the thief. And through his words and acts of kindness, their lives were completely transformed.

Revolutionaries don't presume to know who will respond to disruptive compassion. So they aren't afraid to seize opportunities and hope for positive outcomes.

Joni Eareckson Tada, who became a quadriplegic from a swimming accident, said, "If you truly believe in the value of life, you care about all of the weakest and most vulnerable members of society."[9]

3. You Can't Measure Outcomes without Measuring Yourself

Let's face it: lots of people are in the measuring business. They're quick to tell you what you're doing wrong and where you need to improve. That's why, as a revolutionary, you can't base your success or failure solely on the opinions of others. Rather, listen to people you respect. As crucial as it is to listen to respected outside voices, learn to speak truthfully to yourself. Disruptive compassion is not just about producing outcomes in others; it's also about developing character in yourself. So measure your motives and gauge your morale. Ask yourself the hard questions: How am I really doing? Am I growing? What can I do better?

4. Define Success, Then Measure It

If you saw the film *Moneyball* or you follow Major League Baseball, you'll recall the story of the 2002 Oakland A's. The team, with a limited payroll, decided to reject traditional methods. Rather than relying on managerial intuition and scouting reports to make player decisions, they introduced a new standard of measurement. They assembled a team based on player statistics and their predictive success. Baseball managers, scouts, and sports reporters scoffed at their system. "They're a team of no-names—they won't win," they said. Well, they were wrong. That year, the team won twenty straight games and a division title.

As a revolutionary, you use a different standard for measuring success. You don't base decisions solely on what other people think or what's been done in the past. That will only hold you and your mission back. Tradition says, "Follow the crowd." Disruptive compassion says, "Just do the right thing." Success isn't defined by what's dazzling, loud, and flashy. Success is making the most of opportunities to practice disruptive compassion. It's being kind when a coworker is rude. It's speaking up when a classmate is bullied. It's sending a gift to an impoverished kid when you don't have to. Success is doing the little things in a world with big problems. It's doing your part to move the needle away from hatred toward compassion.

Jim Collins said, "Big does not equal great, and great does not equal big."[10] Too often we measure success by the size of our deed rather than the impact on the need. We assume we're making a difference because the audience is cheering and it makes us feel good. But sometimes we confuse activity with productivity. Often the smallest of gestures can produce the greatest results. That's the power of a life led by disruptive compassion.

We all have the right to define success in our own way. Unfortunately, society attempts to impose its definition on us. You may think, for example, that you need to accumulate houses, cars, bank accounts, jobs, degrees, and more. And as cliché as that list may sound, it's not that far off. A survey revealed that the average American needed the following to feel successful: a more expensive home and car, exotic vacations, and a housekeeper.[11] Revolutionaries reject that definition and instead measure success by their impact on the community, nation, and world.

Albert Einstein said, "Try not to become a person of success, but rather try to become a person of value."[12] And it was Ralph Waldo Emerson who said, "Success: to laugh often and much, to win the respect of intelligent people and the affection of children, to earn the appreciation of honest critics and endure the betrayal of false friends, to appreciate beauty, to find the best in others, to leave the world a bit better, whether by a healthy child, a garden patch, or a redeemed social condition; to know even one life has breathed easier because you have lived. This is to have succeeded!"[13]

FACES OF SUCCESS

Metrics matter, but they don't tell the whole story. The full impact of disruptive compassion isn't always reflected on paper. It's seen in the people whose lives are transformed.

Doree and I were invited to share with more than four hundred women in Addis Ababa, Ethiopia, who were enrolled in Convoy of Hope's Women's Empowerment program. Many of them were single mothers who had suffered abuse and abandonment. But upon graduation, they'd launch their own businesses with seed capital provided by Convoy of Hope partners. Their businesses would include restaurants, stores, farming operations, poultry, tailoring, and more. The success rate for the program is 97 percent, and the women have shown themselves to be smart and resourceful. They just needed someone to believe in them enough to invest in their futures.

Following the talk that day, a young woman approached me. "You can't leave until you hear my story," she said. At thirteen, the young woman explained, she was raped by a man who infected her with HIV. Then, to compound her troubles, she contracted leprosy some years later. When her husband left her, she and her three children were forced to fight for survival in the streets. That's where a Convoy of Hope worker found her. But it wasn't long before she was able to enter the jobs training program and her children were enrolled in school.

Wearing tears and a smile, she said, "Now I have my own business. I'm feeding my own kids. And we have our own place to live."

In countries like El Salvador, Tanzania, the Philippines, and Nicaragua, Convoy of Hope experienced similar results. In Nicaragua, one mother of four children graduated from the Women's Empowerment program and began her poultry business with four chickens. Nine months later, she had dozens of chickens and several employees. She was proud to show me her chicken coops and business ledger, saying, "I am saving every month." I congratulated her and asked, "What is your next goal?" She smiled and said, "More chickens and more workers." Given her start, I had every reason to believe her dreams would come true.

Wardell Jackson stepped to the podium at a church in Rocklin, California. He had traveled from Mississippi to eulogize his former third grade teacher, Barry Noonan.

"I never understood what drove Barry to help me," said Wardell. "Throughout my life he kept in contact."

The two had met in 1963 in a school located in a housing project in East Los Angeles. The area was impoverished and riddled with crime. On weekends, Barry (Kirk Noonan's father) would take Wardell and a few other students to the beach, and a lasting friendship was forged.

"He phoned me every month to see how I was doing," recalled Wardell during the funeral. "At the end of every call he would say, 'Wardell, let me pray for you.' Those prayers are the reason I am here today. Growing up I did some bad things and got myself into some really big trouble when I was seventeen. I was facing prison. But Barry asked the judge to permit me to move in with the Noonans—who had five young children. Barry also promised to get me a job and enroll me in college."

The judge agreed. So Barry became Wardell's surrogate father and driver. The young man didn't own a car, so Barry picked him up night after night at the restaurant where he was employed.

Some of the Noonans' neighbors didn't approve of them having a black youth with a criminal past in their home. But the Noonans shrugged their shoulders and kept pouring into Wardell's life.

"Barry and Linda changed the direction of my life," said Wardell, who went on to become an executive chef. "I can never thank them enough for that."

Through disruptive compassion, you can have a lasting effect on people like Wardell. Your kind words and acts of compassion send them a message that they are neither expendable nor a nuisance. Every person is important and deserves to be dignified with a smile, a handshake, and a hug. The impact of your life is measured by the value you place on theirs.

CHAPTER 12

PERSIST AND PIVOT

*If you don't like the road you're walking, start
paving another one.*

—Dolly Parton

To everyone who says nothing good comes from watching
TV—not so fast.

It was unusual to find Kirk Noonan playing couch
potato, but this night was an exception. He flipped on ABC's
Shark Tank and watched as the cofounders of LuminAID, a
Chicago-based company, demonstrated inflatable solar lanterns. During their presentation, they mentioned an interest
in partnering with relief organizations. That piqued Kirk's
interest, but little did he know how providential it would be.

In the aftermath of Hurricane Irma, one million citizens
in Puerto Rico were left without power. A few weeks later,
Hurricane Maria knocked the entire US territory off the
grid, causing $100 billion in damage. It proved to be the sec-
ond largest blackout in history. Maria caused a massive mess.
Communication systems were down, roofs were ripped from

homes, and access to food and water was limited. Many families went months—not weeks, *months*—without power, their air conditioners sitting idle in sweltering heat and humidity. The elderly and hospital patients were especially vulnerable. Meat and dairy products rotted, and gas stations, grocery stores, and restaurants came to a grinding halt.

Convoy's disaster services team leaped into action. They spun up distribution points for food, water, and supplies. In a matter of weeks, more than 7.5 million meals were distributed to 140,000 families. In addition, they distributed thousands of solar lanterns provided by LuminAID. And later ABC sent a media team to Puerto Rico to film a segment for *Shark Tank* on LuminAID's partnership with Convoy of Hope.

When I arrived in San Juan a few days after the hurricane, I understood how important the solar lanterns were. The streets were dark, flooded, and not passable. Everything was pitch black—like outer space.

I toured the island with Pastor Ivan De la Torre, a prominent leader in the Caribbean. With tears in his eyes, he recounted the lives that were lost and widespread destruction.

"How long will Convoy of Hope stay?" he asked.

"We'll stay until the job is done," I assured him.

Neither of us knew how long that would be. But early assessments claimed it would take years. When there are no quick fixes and the end isn't in sight, it can be overwhelming even for the most committed person. The exposure to pain and loss is draining. But of course, compassion revolutionaries persist. They persevere. They keep going.

Amid the many disaster relief organizations that are heroic, there are always a few opportunistic groups promoting themselves as frontline commandos, when in reality they're back-row fundraisers. News reporters and watchdog groups have investigated NGOs (nongovernmental organizations) and discovered that some lacked financial integrity. Although they claimed to practice revolutionary compassion, their actions suggested they had more interest in profit than people. These are the groups that make a hasty exit when the public's attention shifts to another news story and television cameras stop rolling. Yet many reputable relief organizations remain. They stay engaged until the work they promised to do is completed. They aren't driven by money and they're not easily discouraged by obstacles. They've learned to redraw their plans and repeat their efforts until they get it right.

When people see a natural disaster on television, a passion to do something rises up inside them. But then they don't know what to do. They feel detached, helpless, and insignificant. Yet that's precisely the time to launch off the couch and declare, "I can do something."

Sure, that first step could lead to unfamiliar places. But doing nothing is certain to lead to nothing. Send a donation, hold a food drive, sponsor a fundraiser, mobilize your church or community group, make phone calls. You may be fearful of doing the wrong thing, uncertain that your efforts will make the greatest impact, doubtful you have much worth giving. But you can do *something* to show yourself and the world you care.

Mahatma Gandhi said, "It's the action, not the fruit of the action, that's important. You have to do the right thing. It may not be in your power, may not be in your time, that there'll be any fruit. But that doesn't mean you stop doing the right thing. You may never know what results come from your action. But if you do nothing, there will be no result."[1]

What if Martin Luther King Jr. fled the first time his life

was threatened? Or what if George Washington refused to cross the Delaware River when British soldiers were closing in? Revolutionaries expect opposition because they understand that significant change doesn't occur without grit and perseverance. Complacency—the antithesis of disruptive compassion—also threatens to stop would-be revolutionaries in their tracks. It causes a person to bask in the sun of convenient ignorance. It dulls your sense of purpose and perpetuates surrender to the status quo. It isn't merely the absence of progress—no, complacency erodes progress. It fosters an attachment to the usual that robs you and the rest of the world of something better. Don't try to survive mediocrity.[2] You can't. Think of complacency as hypothermia, with an onset of symptoms so gradual you may not even notice until the medical emergency proves fatal.

Plug your ears to the lies of complacency, such as:

- "Things are just fine the way they are."
- "You're only one person—you can't change much of anything."
- "Live your life, have fun, and let someone else deal with it."
- "You have enough on your plate already."
- "That person will be okay—he or she isn't your problem."
- "You don't have enough to offer, anyway."

You were created to care about this planet and all who call it home. Regardless of your age, gender, education, economic status, religion, politics, or vocation, you were born to make a major contribution to the world. Don't settle for impotence when you were made for importance.

Some people want to tell you you're too (fill in the blank) to practice disruptive compassion. *Too young. Too weak. Too unimportant. Too scared. Too old.* Tell those people to go buy themselves a Slurpee and chill out. You can become a revolutionary at any age and *make* it your prime. Achievement has no age limit. Mozart began composing at age five; Shirley Temple starred in her first major feature film at six; Anne Frank was thirteen when she wrote her diary; and gymnast Nadia Comaneci was fourteen when she recorded a perfect ten in the Olympics. Then there's Leonardo Da Vinci, who was fifty-one when he began painting the *Mona Lisa*; Dr. Seuss, who was fifty-three when *The Cat in the Hat* was published (a huge success, considering his first book was rejected twenty-seven times); not to mention J. R. R. Tolkien, who was sixty-two when The Lord of the Rings was published; and Nelson Mandela, who was seventy-six when he became president of South Africa. There's no reason you can't be the next one to shatter a stereotype. Go for it.

PERSIST

The *Oxford English Dictionary* defines persistence as a "firm or obstinate continuance in a course of action in spite of difficulty or opposition."[3] Resisting the status quo invites opposition. It requires energy and perseverance because, on the front lines, wounds and weariness are inevitable. When exhaustion sets in, you have to fight the urge to wave the white flag. Because surrender in the twenty-first century is less about self-preservation and more about self-gratification. When we grow weary, our defenses lower and we allow ourselves to be led by personal desire rather than duty.

At Convoy of Hope, we've learned not to accept

temporary setbacks as failure. And the learning continues. Whether it's community outreaches, the feeding of children, jobs training, disaster response, or agriculture initiatives, we study outcomes and ask ourselves, "How can we do it better?" Nothing is ever perfect, but we can always say it's better. Winston Churchill said, "Success is stumbling from failure to failure with no loss of enthusiasm."[4]

Churchill faced enormous challenges, as depicted in the film *The Darkest Hour*. Two weeks after he became prime minister of the United Kingdom, the German army seized a wide swath of Europe. An estimated 340,000 British troops had to escape at Dunkirk, and their nation's survival was in true peril. Against this backdrop he declared to the nation, "We shall fight on the seas and oceans, we shall fight with growing confidence and strength in the air, we shall defend our island, whatever the cost may be, we shall fight on the beaches, we shall fight on the landing grounds, we shall fight in the fields and in the streets, we shall fight in the hills; we shall never surrender."[5]

You too have a better chance at success if, like Churchill, you decide you will "never, never, never give up." Your influence in the world will be greater when there is no plan B. That's the level of commitment that declares I won't stop working until

- no more children die from malnutrition.
- no more people are infected with AIDS.
- no more women suffer from breast cancer.
- no more children are trafficked.
- no more young people die from drugs.

When retreat is no longer an option, that's when you

know you and your mission have become one. When there's no getting out of the ring, you can train yourself to take the punches. African American activist Marian Wright Edelman said, "You're not obligated to win. You're obligated to keep trying. To do the best you can every day."[6] And author Samuel Johnson said, "If your determination is fixed, I do not counsel you to despair. Few things are impossible to diligence and skill. Great works are performed not by strength, but perseverance."[7]

Revolutionaries persevere, but they also recognize the importance of nurturing grit in others. They set the bar high—demonstrating persistence—so others can follow their example. Author John C. Maxwell said, "One of the burdens of leadership is that as we go, so go the people we lead. Reaching our potential sets an environment for others to reach theirs. . . . Capacity is not the problem: choice and attitude are. If people are willing to choose improvement and change their attitude, the sky is the limit."[8] And it was Paul the apostle who said, "Do as I do" (1 Cor. 11:1 WE). As a revolutionary, you won't be perfect, but you can remain faithful to the mission. Let friends, family members, coworkers, and classmates question your judgment but never your commitment.

Throwing open the curtains in my room at the Hotel Nacional de Cuba in downtown Havana, I discovered why tourists still flock to this magnificent city. At dawn Havana resembles a scene from a postcard. The sun's rays glinted off a tranquil harbor. Palm trees bent in the warm Caribbean breeze. Peeling Spanish colonial architecture declared a glorious past. And huge finned classic automobiles monopolized the roads.

Leaving the hotel, I caught a glimpse of two young boys standing alone on Havana's shore. Arm in arm, they peered out at the vast ocean as if dreaming of Miami seventy miles away. This was the Communist country born out of rebel-leader Fidel Castro's 1959 revolution.

It was Sunday and I asked my guide to drive me to several house churches that dot the city of 2.2 million residents. In 1991, the government ruled that citizens could gather in private homes for church services. The following year, the constitution was amended to read that Cuba was no longer atheistic, but rather a secular state. Great strides had been made toward religious freedom, but even house churches were still registered and monitored by the government.

Mile after mile, the car passed large billboards and murals featuring the faces of national heroes. *I wonder if this is the fulfillment of Castro's dream*, I asked myself, *or did it fail to meet his expectations?*

The streets were crowded with bicycles, motorcycles, taxis, and pedestrians. I noticed a mother carrying a bag of groceries with her three children in tow. Two elderly men were perched on a park bench reading the newspaper, while nearby, kids played catch with a homemade baseball. (I had seen homemade soccer balls, but this was the first baseball.)

Traveling down an ordinary dirt road, we arrived at a house where people were spilling into the street. Some were peering through windows. Others were seated in the yard, content to listen from a distance. I rolled down my window and heard lively music radiating from the house.

"Can you take me to another one?" I asked the driver, hopefully. "I've never seen anything like this."

"On Sunday they're all over the city," he noted.

Moments later, as he predicted, the scene was repeated. Dozens of people gathered around a house, listening intently to a sermon.

"Do you want to go in?" the driver asked.

"*Sí*—let me check it out."

My blond hair tipped them off—I was *not* Cuban. When the sermon concluded, I was ushered to the front to meet the pastor. Through an interpreter, I explained that I was an American journalist in Havana for three days to write a story. He replied, "*Oraremos para tí,*" which means "We want to pray for you." Instantly I was surrounded by men, women, and children. My Spanish was rusty, so I didn't understand everything they prayed, but I felt their compassion. Some things transcend any language barrier. Wiping tears from my eyes, I found myself hugging complete strangers.

I didn't want to leave, but my arrival had already commandeered the service, so I took the opportunity to slip out the back. Settling back in the car, I began to pray silently. *God, I own so much and yet have so little. These people have few possessions and yet have so much. For years, they worshiped in fear. They persevered until laws changed and some religious freedoms were restored. Help me to have that kind of courage and determination to never give up.*

PIVOT

Time and again, revolutionaries demonstrate commitment to their cause by pressing on in the face of opposition. But they also aren't afraid to reconsider their strategies when new realities come to light. When change is what's needed, persevering on the current path is the last thing you want to do. Dr.

King reorganized his peace marches and captured the attention of a nation. And George Washington revised his plans and crossed the Deleware River to make a surprise attack that would turn the Revolutionary War. Effective pivoting is the result of thorough reconnaissance and instinct. It's sensing when opposition and danger are lurking and knowing when to maneuver in a different direction. As a revolutionary, your convictions and mission remain unchanged, but there may be times to pivot and set a new course for success by embracing new strategies and shedding failing ones.

Author Jim Collins said, "Like an artist who pursues both enduring excellence and shocking creativity, great companies foster a productive tension between continuity and change. On the one hand, they adhere to the principles that produced success in the first place, yet on the other hand, they continually evolve, modifying their approach with creative improvements and intelligent adaptation."[9]

That's the key: *intelligent* adaptation. Pivoting for the sake of pivoting is not guaranteed to produce positive results and can lead to mission drift. It is the strategic pivot, made with mission in mind, that can determine if your goals are reached or not. Take, for example, a study that was conducted of thirty-nine technology companies, each valued at $1 billion. In almost every case, greater success was experienced by pivoting from where the business first started to a different product, service, or strategy.[10] Whether in the context of a revolutionary, an explosive startup, a university, or a church, it can be difficult to maintain a willingness to pivot. The more successful you are, the more attached you can become to the *ways* you achieved that success. It's easy to become entrenched and not recognize it.

Why would anyone delay a pivot? Well, there are the

obvious reasons: we dislike change, we fear failure, or we simply don't see the need. It's not difficult to lose touch with reality, convincing ourselves we're making progress when the facts tell a different story. Everyone knows what it's like to miss or ignore the road signs. Whatever the reason for the failure to pivot, the consequences can be catastrophic: businesses file for bankruptcy, charities sacrifice momentum, churches become like morgues, governments lose credibility, and movements die.

In terms of disruptive compassion, pivoting may change *how* you spend your time, *who* you work with, *where* you serve, *what* needs you meet, and *when* you take action. More specifically, it may mean adjusting class schedules so you can volunteer at a church, school, or charity. It may require you to step down from a committee or let go of an extracurricular activity so you can redirect your focus. It may necessitate creating margin in your life so you have more time and energy to respond to the needs around you.

Trust your instincts. You were born with an ability to read situations. If you're a person of faith, naturally you can rely on prayer for guidance. But don't doubt yourself. Chances are, you'll know exactly what you need to do next.

CHAPTER 13

GO

Stop chasing the money and start chasing the passion.

—Tony Hsieh

As our Land Rover crossed the border from Uzbekistan into Afghanistan, our driver hollered a warning: "Too many landmines—need to drive in the riverbeds." Abandoned tanks and military vehicles were like billboards advertising a war zone. *Like I need a reminder.* In the distance I could see plumes of smoke and hear the rapid cadence of gunfire.

"Say a prayer!" our driver called, veering abruptly onto a dirt road up the side of the mountain. I wasn't sure if he was warning of landmines or sniper fire, but I figured my prayer was intense enough to cover both. Like an ascending roller coaster, our vehicle climbed at a 45-degree angle to a remote village. Below, in the riverbed, we had guzzled bottles of water in 95-degree heat, but up here heavy snow was falling. The contrast was nearly as jarring as the ride. When we arrived, shoeless children encircled our Land Rover, their shivering faces lipstick purple.

All at once, the crowd parted and the village chief stepped forward, greeting us with his hand on his heart and a respectful nod. Through an interpreter, he said, "Welcome to our village."

We smiled and bowed our heads, but I still wondered if he was sympathetic to extremists.

He led us atop a large rock overlooking a hillside covered with small mounds of fresh dirt. "These are graves of our children. Without help, many will follow," he said, stone faced but with deep sorrow in his eyes. "Already we eat next year's seed to survive—we have nothing left."

If we don't help them, his prophecy will come to fruition, I told myself. *If we don't put shoes on the children and give them coats, they won't make it.* There wasn't time for a debate about long-term sustainability, economic impact, or capturing a good story. This was a rescue mission. They needed our help now or they wouldn't survive the winter. That day we formulated a relief plan and pledged to return with aid. In gratitude, the chief and village elders clasped their hands and bowed at the waist.

Descending the mountain, I glanced at the dozens of hillside graves one last time. My mind flashed back to when I was twelve, standing over my dad's grave. "God, why did he have to die?" I asked then. Now, from the back seat of a Land Rover, I found myself asking the same question: *Why did these children have to suffer and die?*

My mind flashed to childhood memories of neighbors and churchgoers ringing our doorbell and delivering bags of groceries. We never broadcasted that our cupboards were empty, but repeatedly people arrived just in time. My siblings and I tore into those grocery bags like explorers seeking lost treasure, hoping for a box of Froot Loops or a Hershey's bar.

The Land Rover continued to crawl down the mountain. I was lost in my thoughts, hardly noticing the ominous cliffs and absence of guardrails. So we rode in silence. I'm not sure if it was God speaking to me or just my imagination, but these words rang in my head: *Hal, who do you think sent those neighbors to your door? I did. And how do you think you discovered this village? I brought you here. If you do your part, I'll do mine.*

I still had many unanswered questions, but for the first time I felt like I was shaking hands with God. I knew he wanted to help the poor and suffering more than I did; he was just looking for willing partners. I wasn't sure how this would play out in my everyday life, but I had a strong suspicion disruptive compassion would be a major part of it.

Two days later, a truck filled with food, coats, shoes, and seed arrived in the village. The people were spared more heartache, but my place in the world also came into focus on that mountain. As much as I wanted to blame someone—anyone—for the world's problems, deep down I knew I was wasting my breath. I needed to keep my eyes on *my* mission and do the next kind thing in front of *me*.

The earth will never be Eden, no matter what we do. But it can be better. And if we can make it better, there isn't a good reason not to try. It's time to go for it—for each of us to practice disruptive compassion and usher in a revolution of kindness.

Where do you want *your* life to go? Maybe you're not sure. I know for a long time I wasn't. Some days I still have questions. And that's okay. The direction is more important than the destination. Perhaps you feel like you've been wandering aimlessly for some time. Maybe you've even been reading this book, thinking, *I just need to travel somewhere and break out of my bubble—that will fix everything.* I hate to break it to you, but randomly flying to some place like Samoa or Moldova won't put an end to your search for greater meaning. Instead, the disruptive compassion you practice today—right where you are—can provide the course correction you're looking for. That doesn't mean there won't be times when hopping on a plane is exactly what you should do. Saying yes to an opportunity outside your comfort zone could lead to greater clarity and inspiration.

But how do you navigate all this? It starts with a decision to abandon a me-first fantasy and accept the role of a revolutionary. No one wants to look back and regret trading significance for a boring, self-centered life. That doesn't have to be your story. You may be telling yourself, *It's too late to change my routine. My life is too complicated. I don't have that much to offer the world anyway.* If you write yourself off, you're writing others off too. There are people who won't receive help because you didn't make disruptive compassion a priority. I'm not trying to lay a guilt trip on you—it's just a fact. No excuses—just go for it. Actor Jim Carrey said it well: "You can fail at what you don't want, so you might as well take a chance on doing what you love."[1]

FOUR STEPS TOWARD FULFILLING YOUR MISSION

Here are four steps you can take to disrupt your life and begin fulfilling *your* mission.

1. Reject the Status Quo
If everyone lived the way you do, would the world be a better place? If not, then quite frankly, you have some work to do. As a revolutionary, you'll begin to see money, work,

friendships, and other resources differently. Your life will collide with the status quo. Tell yourself, "The way things are now is not the way things are going to be." You must "kill your status quo before it kills you."[2]

When you embark on a life of disruptive compassion, you're leaving your comfort zone behind. Comfort zones stunt growth, preventing you from experiencing new things and causing you to settle for less than the best. Most people procrastinate doing things outside their comfort zone. A way to combat that is to make a list of things you're putting off and tackle them one at a time.

But maybe procrastination isn't your vice. Maybe you find it difficult to break out of your comfort zone. Take a risk. Take a baby step. Go somewhere new or talk to someone you don't know. Give a helping hand to a family member or friend. Do something unexpected for a neighbor. Make a generous donation to a community project. Baby steps—you might be surprised how far they take you on the trailhead to fulfillment and purpose.

Sheryl Sandberg, chief operating officer at Facebook, asked, "What would you do if you weren't afraid?"[3] Some would rather work to convince themselves they're happy and fulfilled than explore what else life has to offer. If they could see past their fears, they'd see the adventure called disruptive compassion. We are often our own worst enemy; we are our greatest obstacle. We self-sabotage. We limit our potential. We divert our attention away from what matters most. It's time to reject the status quo and go for it.

2. Live Your Manifesto

There's great value in writing a personal mission statement or manifesto, because then *you* know what it is. But knowing your manifesto is pointless if it lives only on the page. Take it one step farther; make the decision to *live* your manifesto. You may want to begin by making a list of your life goals. You are capable of great things, but it helps to be realistic. Don't write that you're going to be a brain surgeon if you aren't intending to go to medical school. Or don't aspire to play center for the Golden State Warriors if you're fully grown at five-foot-three. Remember, your manifesto is less about your vocation or location and more about your devotion to your mission. Are you prepared to be a revolutionary who takes responsibility for making your world a better place? If so, say *that* in your manifesto. Don't hesitate to dream about the *kind* of person you want to be and the kind of world you want to help create.

Possessing a vision is critical to fulfillment and happiness. "Where there is no vision, the people perish" (Prov. 29:18 KJV). In business—or even a movement of compassion—a vision gives purpose. "Without purpose, people get lost, distracted, focus on things that don't matter in the long run, or completely disengage," said one author. He analyzed the vision statements of *Forbes*'s top-ten valuable brands, including the following:

- Facebook: "To bring the world closer together."
- Google: "To organize the world's information and make it universally accessible and useful."
- GE: "To build, power, cure, move, and connect the world."
- Microsoft: "Empower every person and every organization on the planet to achieve more."
- Toyota: "To enrich lives around the world with the safest and most responsible ways of moving people."[4]

These vision statements are aspirational, outwardly focused, inspiring, realistic, clear, and concise. Likewise, your manifesto should be hopeful and ambitious. It should be so compelling that you wake up each morning determined to live out your mission. Make sure it's one of the first things you read every day by posting it on your bathroom mirror, refrigerator, or coffee maker.

3. Lead by Example

By practicing disruptive compassion, you can create a ripple of goodness that inspires others and generates hope. When others observe your life, hopefully they see character traits that make you the kind of revolutionary they want to follow. They admire your consistency, generosity, kindness, selflessness, mercy, work ethic, reliability, patience, and optimism. And admiration often leads to emulation.

4. Finish the Task

In a Kenyan slum, more than a thousand students stood in line to receive lunch at school. I watched from the schoolyard, thankful that Convoy of Hope was feeding the children and helping to ensure they received an education. We had learned that feeding children in school increased attendance. Because of the meal, parents were more inclined to send their children to school rather than having them beg on street corners or scavenge off garbage heaps to help support the family.

When I glanced at the exterior of the schoolyard, however, I noticed dozens of eyes peering through the fence. When I walked outside the gate, they came running. Instantly my heart broke. *These kids are probably sniffing glue to take away their hunger,* I told myself. *Feeding a thousand children isn't enough. We have to find a way to get them inside the schoolyard, on the other side of the fence. Our job isn't done—we have to do more.*

Revolutionaries live with a sense of urgency. We can't rely on yesterday's accomplishments to justify today's inaction. How can we when children are dying, women are trafficked, and refugees are fleeing? We're determined to spend more of ourselves so others can be rescued. As revolutionaries, we're the ones who befriend students who were ostracized, drop off bags of groceries to families in need, place phone calls to people who suffered a disappointment, visit inmates and senior citizens, empty our purses and wallets to feed hungry children, and more. There is no end game. Our task is to defeat hopelessness with disruptive compassion. We may be only one revolutionary, but together with other revolutionaries, we believe we can change the world.

Steve Jobs said, "Your time is limited, so don't waste it living someone else's life. Don't be trapped by dogma—which is living with the results of other people's thinking. Don't let the noise of others' opinions drown out your own inner voice. And most important, have the courage to follow your heart and intuition. They somehow already know what you truly want to become. Everything else is secondary."[5] There are times when "following your heart" (or obeying God's voice) means choosing defiance over compliance. You have to do what's right rather than what's popular. As musical artist Lauren Daigle said, "I definitely don't ever plan on compromising, and if that means I'm rebellious, then so be it. I'm all for it."[6]

Your life is a novel with many chapters. Regardless of your age or stage in life, you can write the rest of the story. Remember the line from Pixar's *Ratatouille*: "Not everyone can become a great artist, but a great artist can come from anywhere." You are not limited and confined by where you've come from or where you've been. The laptop is in your hands. Your story can be filled with new adventures and seized opportunities. And fortunately, you don't have to take this journey alone. God is with you—showing you people along the way who need a helping hand and a message of hope. May your life be punctuated by the lives you served, the people you influenced, and the status quos you challenged. And when the final page is written and the cover is closed, may it be subtitled *The Life and Times of a Modern-Day Revolutionary.*

EPILOGUE

My daughter Lindsay, Kevin Rose, and I were visiting program centers in Haiti when we arrived at an orphanage. I was amazed by the transformation of the facilities in just one year's time. When Convoy of Hope and a partner organization, Mission of Hope, began working there, the orphanage's cooks were preparing meals over an open fire, using an outhouse for a toilet, and in need of beds and desks for the children. Now they had a formal kitchen, a washroom, new mattresses, and remodeled, kid-friendly classrooms. The work had been accomplished through field teams, groups of volunteers who had come from all over the United States.

As the orphanage director showed us the new facilities, a small boy with a wide smile wrapped his arms around my waist. He wouldn't let go. At times it felt as though we were in a three-legged race.

When it was time to leave, it was both physically and emotionally difficult to unfasten myself from that determined little boy. I knew I couldn't stay, and as our Jeep pulled away, I locked eyes with him one last time. He was crying. The director was trying to console him but to no avail. I'm pretty sure he thought I was going to be his friend forever, and now I was leaving without him.

We drove away in silence for a mile or two before I spoke up. "I wish we could take every child in this orphanage home with us, but we can't. So we have to do the next best thing. And that is to make sure as many children as possible grow up healthy and educated. We have to make sure every child is given a future and the terrorists can't buy their souls for a bowl of rice."

Lindsay and Kevin nodded.

More silence.

I said to myself, *We're feeding two hundred thousand children a day now, but how amazing it would be to have the resources to play a part in feeding and educating one million children each day. That would ensure they grow up to be the right kind of revolutionary: the ones who change their country and the world.*

As we wrote earlier in this book, and certainly as we all know by now, the world doesn't need "tweaking." It needs profound change. It needs a revolution marked by disruptive compassion.

This is no small task. Fortunately, it's simple enough for each of us to do our part. We hope you'll hear this good news: *you* possess the power to provoke change and rally people to a united act of compassion. And *you* can make a radical difference through disruptive compassion, wherever you are.

The following manifesto has helped remind us to make the choice for disruptive compassion every day. Our great hope is that it can do the same for you.

HOPE REFUSE TO LOSE IT.

THE WORLD IS HURTING BUT **SOMETHING** CAN ALWAYS BE DONE.

THE STATUS QUO IS OVERRATED BETTER IS **BETTER** POSSIBLE IS POSSIBLE.

SACRIFICE IS NOT A BURDEN.

ALWAYS DO THE NEXT KIND THING.

LOVE SIMPLY — GOD, PEOPLE, PLANET.

TOMORROW DOESN'T EXCUSE TODAY IT DEPENDS ON IT.

BE IMPATIENT & INTOLERANT (FOR JUSTICE) (OF HATRED)

EXPECT OBSTACLES AND **KEEP GOING.**

BECOME A REVOLUTIONARY.

DISRUPTIVE COMPASSION *manifesto*

NOTES

Introduction

1. Matt Seybold, "The Apocryphal Twain: The Two Most Important Days of Your Life," Center for Mark Twain Studies, December 6, 2016, http://marktwainstudies.com/the-apocryphal -twain-the-two-most-important-days-of-your-life/.
2. William P. Barnett, "Why You Don't Understand Disruption," Stanford Graduate School of Business, March 7, 2017, https:// www.gsb.stanford.edu/insights/why-you-dont-understand -disruption.

Chapter 1: Believe

1. "Lessons of Steve Jobs: Guy Kawasaki at TEDxUCSD," YouTube video, 18:41, posted by TEDx Talks on June 4, 2013, https:// www.youtube.com/watch?v=rWv-KoZnpKw.
2. "Arnold Toynbee: British Historian," *Encyclopaedia Britannica Online*, accessed September 12, 2018, https://www.britannica .com/biography/Arnold-Joseph-Toynbee.
3. Elizabeth Dori Tunstall, "Un-designing Apathy: Designs for Systems of Caring," *The Conversation*, February 5, 2014, http://theconversation.com/un-designing-apathy-designs-for -systems-of-caring-22866.
4. Allen Tappe, *The Power of Purposed Performance: Choosing to Live Your Life on Purpose*, 2nd ed. (Arlington, TX: Institute for Purposed Performance, 2003), 31.

5. Charles R. Swindoll, *Swindoll's Ultimate Book of Illustrations and Quotes: Over 1,500 Ways to Effectively Drive Home Your Message* (Nashville: Thomas Nelson, 2003), 115.

6. Sonia K., "Holocaust Survivor: This Is Not the America I Came To," CNN, August 21, 2017, https://www.cnn.com/2017/08/19/opinions/holocaust-survivor-trump-charlottesville-sonia-k-opinion/index.html.

7. Clint Smith, "The Danger of Silence," TED, July 2014, https://www.ted.com/talks/clint_smith_the_danger_of_silence/transcript.

8. Natasha Puri, "The Apathy Epidemic," *HuffPost*, April 28, 2016, https://www.huffingtonpost.com/natasha-puri/the-apathy-epidemic_b_9797624.html.

Chapter 2: Define the Mission

1. Grammarly, "How to Write Your Manifesto in Five Steps," *HuffPost*, July 11, 2014, https://www.huffingtonpost.com/grammarly/write-manifesto_b_5575496.html.

2. Matt Valentine, "Three Reasons Your Comfort Zone Is Killing You (and How to Beat It)," *GoalCast*, August 22, 2017, https://www.goalcast.com/2017/08/22/comfort-zone-killing-you-how-to-beat-it/.

3. Hilary Tindle, *Up: How Positive Outlook Can Transform Our Health and Aging* (New York: Hudson Street Press, 2013), 69.

4. Scott Keyes, "Everything You Think You Know about Panhandlers Is Wrong," *ThinkProgress*, October 30, 2013, https://thinkprogress.org/everything-you-think-you-know-about-panhandlers-is-wrong-36b41487730d/.

5. Chris Walker, "Homelessness in Denver: The Cold, Hard Facts behind Six Myths," *Westword.com*, December 4, 2016, https://www.westword.com/news/homelessness-in-denver-the-cold-hard-facts-behind-six-myths-7348310.

6. Katherine W. Phillips, "How Diversity Makes Us Smarter: Being around People Who Are Different from Us Makes Us

More Creative, More Diligent, and Harder-Working," *Scientific American*, October 1, 2014, https://www.scientificamerican.com/article/how-diversity-makes-us-smarter/.

7. Danah Boyd, "Self-Segregation: How a Personalized World Is Dividing Americans," *The Guardian*, January 13, 2017, https://www.theguardian.com/technology/2017/jan/13/self-segregation-military-facebook-college-diversity.

8. Charles R. Swindoll, *Swindoll's Ultimate Book of Illustrations and Quotes: Over 1,500 Ways to Effectively Drive Home Your Message* (Nashville: Thomas Nelson, 2003), 360.

Chapter 3: Do Reconnaissance

1. "Social Mobility: Crash Course Sociology #26," YouTube video, 9:01, posted by CrashCourse on September 25, 2017, https://www.youtube.com/watch?v=GjuV-XdYHhA.

2. History.com Editors, "Sun Tzu," *History.com*, accessed September 12, 2018, https://www.history.com/topics/sun-tzu.

3. *Merriam-Webster*, s.v. "reconnaissance," accessed September 12, 2018, https://www.merriam-webster.com/dictionary/reconnaissance.

4. Christopher Small, "Adrien Brody Is Still Haunted by *The Pianist* after Fifteen Years," IndieWire, August 7, 2017, https://www.indiewire.com/2017/08/adrien-brody-interview-the-pianist-locarno-film-festival-1201864271/.

Chapter 4: Conduct an Audit

1. Greg Satell and Srdja Popovic, "How Protests Become Successful Social Movements," *Harvard Business Review*, January 27, 2017, https://hbr.org/2017/01/how-protests-become-successful-social-movements.

2. Samantha Olson, "Scientists Develop New Parkinsons Disease Drug Treatment That Attacks Symptoms on Two Fronts," *Medical Daily*, June 21, 2013, https://www.medicaldaily.com/

    scientists-develop-new-parkinsons-disease-drug-treatment
    -attacks-symptoms-two-fronts-247042.

3. America's Charities, "Facts and Statistics on Workplace Giving, Matching Gifts, and Volunteer Programs," *Charities.org*, accessed September 12, 2018, https://www.charities.org/facts-statistics -workplace-giving-matching-gifts-and-volunteer-programs.

4. Ibid.

5. Jay Buys, "Why B Corporations Matter," *Thisisvisceral.com*, February 22, 2018, https://www.thisisvisceral.com/2018/02/ b-corporations-matter.

6. Robert F. Kennedy, "Day of Affirmation Address (News Release Version), University of Capetown, Capetown, South Africa, June 6, 1966," John F. Kennedy Presidential Library and Museum, accessed September 12, 2018, https://www.jfklibrary.org/ Research/Research-Aids/Ready-Reference/RFK-Speeches/Day -of-Affirmation-Address-news-release-text-version.aspx.

7. Ellie Kemper, "A Few Thoughts on the Male Anatomy from Ellie Kemper," *GQ*, April 9, 2016, https://www.gq.com/ story/a-few-thoughts-on-the-male-anatomy-from-ellie-kemper.

Chapter 5: Be Authentic

1. "Chapter 20: The Minister in a Maze," SparkNotes, accessed September 12, 2018, http://www.sparknotes.com/nofear/lit/ the-scarlet-letter/chapter-20/.

2. "It Is Better to Fail in Originality, Than to Succeed in Imitation: #MondayMotivation," *SmallBusiness.com*, accessed September 13, 2018, https://smallbusiness.com/monday-morning-motivation/ failure-is-the-true-test-of-greatness/.

3. Marty Neumeier, *ZAG: The Number One Strategy of High-Performance Brands* (Berkeley, CA: New Riders, 2007), 147.

4. "Sam Harris Extended Interview," *Religion and Ethics Newsweekly*, January 5, 2007, http://www.pbs.org/wnet/religionandethics/ 2007/01/05/january-5-2007-sam-harris-extended-interview/ 3736/.

Chapter 6: Build a Team

1. "Forty-Five Inspiring Quotes about Teamwork," *The Quotes Master*, accessed June 18, 2018, http://thequotesmaster.com/2015/12/45-inspiring-quotes-about-team-work/.

2. ZAZA, "The Strength of the TEAM Is Each Individual Member. The Strength of Each Member Is the TEAM!" *Medium*, March 4, 2018, https://medium.com/@ZAZA.WORLD/the-strength-of-the-team-is-each-individual-member-the-strength-of-each-member-is-the-team-b2aca167f230.

3. Edmond Lau, "Why and Where Is Teamwork Important?" *Forbes*, January 23, 2013, https://www.forbes.com/sites/quora/2013/01/23/why-and-where-is-teamwork-important/#611243c3287a.

4. Alejandro Crawford, "What Business Schools Could Learn from *Ocean's Eleven*: Students Need Experience Collaborating with People in Other Disciplines and Fields," *U.S. News and World Report*, November 26, 2013, https://www.usnews.com/opinion/blogs/economic-intelligence/2013/11/26/what-business-schools-could-learn-from-oceans-eleven-and-the-hobbit.

5. Robert Passikoff, "Freeing the Lincoln Brand," *Forbes*, December 4, 2012, https://www.forbes.com/sites/marketshare/2012/12/04/freeing-the-lincoln-brand/#44d98b7d8bb4.

6. Leon Logothetis, "Keeping Good Company: Why You Should Surround Yourself with Good People," *HuffPost*, March 6, 2015, https://www.huffingtonpost.com/leon-logothetis/kkeeping-good-company-why-you-should-surround-yourself-with-good-people_b_6816468.html.

7. Dave Kerpen, "Fifteen Quotes to Inspire Great Teamwork: The Difference between Success and Failure Is a Great Team. Here's How to Inspire Yours," *Inc.com*, accessed September 12, 2018, https://www.inc.com/dave-kerpen/15-quotes-to-inspire-great-team-work.html?cid=search.

8. "Forty-Five Inspiring Quotes," *Quotes Master*.

9. Ibid.

Chapter 7: Pay the Invoice

1. "English Word with the Most Meanings," *Guinness World Records*, accessed September 13, 2018, http://www.guinnessworldrecords. com/world-records/english-word-with-the-most-meanings/.

2. "What Is Generosity?" *Science of Generosity*, University of Notre Dame College of Arts and Letters, accessed September 13, 2018, https://generosityresearch.nd.edu/more-about-the-initiative/ what-is-generosity/.

3. Ibid.

4. Joshua Becker, "Nine Ways Generous People See the World Differently," *Becoming Minimalist*, accessed September 13, 2018, https://www.becomingminimalist.com/more-generosity/.

5. Amanda Macmillan, "Being Generous Really Does Make You Happier," *Time*, July 14, 2017, http://time.com/4857777/ generosity-happiness-brain/.

6. John Wesley, "The Use of Money," *Global Ministries: The United Methodist Church*, accessed September 13, 2018, https://www .umcmission.org/Find-Resources/John-Wesley-Sermons/ Sermon-50-The-Use-of-Money.

7. "The Five Love Languages," *The 5 Love Languages*, accessed September 13, 2018, https://www.5lovelanguages.com.

Chapter 8: Create Momentum

1. CNN Library, "Hurricane Katrina Statistics Fast Facts," *CNN*, updated August 30, 2018, https://www.cnn.com/2013/08/23/ us/hurricane-katrina-statistics-fast-facts/index.html. Office for Coastal Management, "Fast Facts: Hurricane Costs," National Oceanic and Atmospheric Administration, accessed September 13, 2018, https://coast.noaa.gov/states/fast-facts/hurricane-costs.html.

2. Ben Cosgrove, "Gandhi and His Spinning Wheel: The Story behind an Iconic Photo," *Time*, September 10, 2014, http:// time.com/3639043/gandhi-and-his-spinning-wheel-the-story -behind-an-iconic-photo/.

3. John Centofanti, "Four Reasons to Avoid Negative Marketing

Messages," *Creative Stream Marketing*, October 18, 2014, https:// creativestreammarketing.com/4-reasons-to-avoid-negative -marketing-messages/.

4. Anthony Moore, "Short-Term Intensity vs. Long-Term Consistency," *Medium*, January 19, 2017, https://medium .com/@anthony_moore/short-term-intensity-vs-long-term -consistency-440e6060ce81.

5. Anthony Moore, "Fourteen Principles You Must Master to Become Successful," *Medium*, August 10, 2017, https://medium .com/the-mission/14-principles-you-must-master-to-become -successful-d3387517ab5.

6. Jonny Miller, "Will Smith's Philosophy," *Medium*, March 24, 2013, https://medium.com/@jonnym1ller/will-smiths -philosophy-668f37dd51b1.

7. John Brubaker, "Forget Big Goals. Take Baby Steps for Small, Daily Wins," *Entrepreneur*, January 14, 2015, https://www .entrepreneur.com/article/241754.

8. Misha, "The Power of Momentum: And How to Jump Off the Treadmill without Breaking Your Leg," *Medium*, July 2, 2018, https://medium.com/@mishablog/the-power-of -momentum-22cd226adf05.

9. Adam Braun, "The Importance of #IamMalala on November 10th," *HuffPost*, November 8, 2012, https://www.huffingtonpost .com/adam-braun/malala-day_b_2092721.html.

10. George Bradt, "IBM's Sue Hed Shows How Early Wins Get You Ahed [sic] of the Curve," *Forbes*, March 30, 2011, https://www .forbes.com/sites/georgebradt/2011/03/30/ibms-sue-hed-shows -how-early-wins-get-you-ahed-of-the-curve/#3fb1cc0d6618.

11. George Bradt, "Warning: Early Wins for New Leaders Can Be Counterproductive," *Forbes*, March 28, 2012, https://www .forbes.com/sites/georgebradt/2012/03/28/warning-early-wins -for-new-leaders-can-be-counterproductive/#292065e36088.

12. Ken Miyamoto, "Screenwriting Advice from SOLO Director Ron Howard," *Screencraft*, May 25, 2018, https://screencraft

.org/2018/05/25/screenwriting-advice-from-solo-director
-ron-howard/.

Chapter 9: Eliminate Distractions

1. TED Partners, "The Distracted Mind," TED-Ed: Lessons Worth
Sharing, accessed September 13, 2018, https://ed.ted.com/
featured/Lj5N4g31#watch.
2. Mike Vardy, "Three Things to Help You Get Your Focus Back
When You've Lost It," *Productivityist.com*, accessed September 13,
2018, https://productivityist.com/3-things-get-focus-back/.
3. Antonio Tijerino, "Texts Cause Wrecks," *Fox News*, May 1,
2013, http://www.foxnews.com/opinion/2013/05/01/texts-cause
-wrecks-and-can-wait.html.
4. Rajan Kaicker, "Four Steps to Clarify Your Goals and Reach
the Finish Line," *Linkedin*, January 6, 2015, https://www
.linkedin.com/pulse/4-steps-clarify-your-goals-reach-finish
-line-rajan-kaicker.
5. Chris McChesney, Sean Covey, and Jim Huling, *The Four
Disciplines of Execution: Achieving Your Wildly Important Goals*
(New York: Free Press, 2012).
6. Stephanie Vozza, "The Real Reason Why You're Easily
Distracted Has Nothing to Do with Technology," *Fast Company*,
July 28, 2017, https://www.fastcompany.com/40442595/
the-real-reason-why-youre-easily-distracted-has-nothing-to
-do-with-technology.
7. Nerisha Penrose, "A Day-by-Day Breakdown of Kanye West's
Headline-Grabbing Return to Twitter," *Billboard*, April 26, 2018,
https://www.billboard.com/articles/columns/hip-hop/8390268/
kanye-west-twitter-trump-new-music-john-legend.
8. Mail Online, "Simon Cowell: I'm Quite Odd, I Have Dark
Moods," *HuffPost*, updated May 25, 2011, https://www
.huffingtonpost.com/2009/05/24/simon-cowell-im-quite
-odd_n_207140.html.

9. "Thoughts on the Business of Life," *ForbesQuotes*, accessed September 13, 2018, https://www.forbes.com/quotes/3974/.

10. John Lee Dumas, "Lack of Direction, Not Lack of Time, Is the Problem," *Medium*, September 12, 2016, https://medium.com/@johnleedumas/lack-of-direction-not-lack-of-time-is-the-problem-a419a7e64bd2.

11. "The Success Principles: Twelve-Month Success Planner," Jack Canfield, accessed September 13, 2018, http://jackcanfield.com/success/op/12-month-success-planner.html.

Chapter 10: Take Risks

1. Mitch Ditkoff, "Fifty Awesome Quotes on Risk Taking," *HuffPost*, November 8, 2012, https://www.huffingtonpost.com/entry/50-awesome-quotes-on-risk_b_2078573.html.

2. Ibid.

3. Paul Hudson, "The Biggest Risk Is Not Taking One: Fourteen Risks Everyone Needs to Take in Life," *Elite Daily*, April 8, 2014, https://www.elitedaily.com/life/motivation/14-risks-everyone-needs-take-life.

4. Ibid.

5. Jason Fell, "As Mark Zuckerberg Turns Thirty, His Ten Best Quotes as CEO," *Entrepreneur*, May 14, 2014, https://www.entrepreneur.com/article/233890.

6. Ditkoff, "Fifty Awesome Quotes."

7. Ibid.

8. Ibid.

9. Ibid.

10. Margie Warrell, "Take a Risk: The Odds Are Better Than You Think," *Forbes*, June 18, 2013, https://www.forbes.com/sites/margiewarrell/2013/06/18/take-a-risk-the-odds-are-better-than-you-think/#763b705845c2.

11. "Thirty Compassion Quotes to Offer Companionship through Suffering," *Aimhappy.com*, November 24, 2017, https://aimhappy.com/compassion-quotes-suffering/.

12. Ditkoff, "Fifty Awesome Quotes."

13. Derek Sivers, "How to Start a Movement," TED2010, February 2010, https://www.ted.com/talks/derek_sivers _how_to_start_a_movement.

14. Guy Kawasaki, "The Art of Innovation—TEDxBerkeley," YouTube video, 21:15, posted by TEDx Talks on February 22, 2014, https://www.youtube.com/watch?v=Mtjatz9r-Vc.

15. Ditkoff, "Fifty Awesome Quotes."

Chapter 11: Measure Outcomes

1. Dean Karlan and Jacob Appel, *More Than Good Intentions: Improving the Ways the World's Poor Borrow, Save, Farm, Learn, and Stay Healthy* (New York: Plume, 2011), 27–31, 270–71.

2. Abhijit Banerjee and Esther Duflo, *Poor Economics: A Radical Rethinking of the Way to Fight Global Poverty* (New York: PublicAffairs, 2011).

3. Deborah Mills-Scofield, "It's Not Just Semantics: Managing Outcomes vs. Outputs," *Harvard Business Review*, November 26, 2012, https://hbr.org/2012/11/its-not-just -semantics-managing-outcomes.

4. Ibid.

5. Ben Yoskovitz, "Measuring What Matters: How to Pick a Good Metric," *OnStartups.com*, March 29, 2013, http://www.onstartups .com/tabid/3339/bid/96738/Measuring-What-Matters-How-To -Pick-A-Good-Metric.aspx.

6. Jed Emerson, Jay Wachowicz, and Suzi Chun, "Social Return on Investment (SROI): Exploring Aspects of Value Creation," Harvard Business School Working Knowledge: Business Research for Business Leaders, January 29, 2001, https://hbswk.hbs.edu/ archive/social-return-on-investment-sroi-exploring-aspects-of -value-creation. Accessed August 3, 2018.

7. Frank Partnoy, "The Cost of a Human Life, Statistically Speaking: Is There Any Satisfactory Method for Assessing the True Cost

of a Human Life?" *The Globalist*, July 21, 2012, https://www
.theglobalist.com/the-cost-of-a-human-life-statistically-speaking.

8. Ivette K. Caballero, "Thirty Great Quotes about the Value
of Life," *Linkedin*, May 31, 2015, https://www.linkedin.com/
pulse/30-great-quotes-value-life-ivette-k-caballero.

9. Ibid.

10. Jim Collins, *How the Mighty Fall: And Why Some Companies Never
Give In* (New York: HarperCollins, 2009), 54.

11. "The American Idea of Success," *Discover Bank*, accessed
September 13, 2018, https://www.discover.com/credit-cards/
resources/the-american-idea-of-success/.

12. "Success Quotes," Jeroen De Flander, updated February 25, 2018,
https://jeroen-de-flander.com/success-quotes/.

13. Nick Scheidies, "Fifty Great Thoughts on Success," *Income*,
accessed September 13, 2018, https://www.incomediary.com/
50-great-thoughts-on-success.

Chapter 12: Persist and Pivot

1. Ashoka, "Twelve Great Quotes from Gandhi on His Birthday,"
Forbes, October 2, 2012, https://www.forbes.com/sites/
ashoka/2012/10/02/12-great-quotes-from-gandhi-on-his
-birthday/#1942e8b633d8.

2. Caroline O'Connor and Perry Klebahn, "The Strategic Pivot:
Rules for Entrepreneurs and Other Innovators," *Harvard
Business Review*, February 28, 2011, https://hbr.org/2011/02/
how-and-when-to-pivot-rules-fo.

3. *Oxford Dictionaries*, s.v. "persistence," accessed September 13, 2018,
https://en.oxforddictionaries.com/definition/us/persistence.

4. "Top Twenty-Four Winston Churchill Quotes to Inspire You to
Never Surrender," *Goalcast*, June 20, 2017, https://www.goalcast
.com/2017/06/20/top-24-winston-churchill-quotes-to-inspire
-you-to-never-surrender/.

5. Geoff Loftus, "If You're Going through Hell, Keep Going—
Winston Churchill," *Forbes*, May 9, 2012, https://www.forbes

.com/sites/geoffloftus/2012/05/09/if-youre-going-through
-hell-keep-going-winston-churchill/#103a5aeed549.

6. Jone Johnson Lewis, "Marian Wright Edelman Quotes,"
   ThoughtCo., updated March 11, 2017, https://www.thoughtco
   .com/marian-wright-edelman-quotes-3530138.

7. James A. Middleton, Michael A. Tallman, Neil Hatfield, and
   Owen Davis, "Taking the Severe out of Perseverance: Strategies
   for Building Mathematical Determination," Arizona State
   University, April 2015, https://www.spencer.org/sites/default/
   files/pdfs/middleton_tallman_hatfield_davis_mip_0415.pdf.

8. John C. Maxwell, *The Five Levels of Leadership* (New York: Center
   Street, 2011), 17.

9. Jim Collins, *How the Mighty Fall: And Why Some Companies Never
   Give In* (New York: HarperCollins, 2009), 36.

10. Steve Blank, "Why Pivots Are Pivotal to Your Success,"
    Think Growth, August 30, 2017, https://thinkgrowth.org/
    why-pivots-are-pivotal-to-your-success-93467c40e8a.

Chapter 13: Go

1. "Jim Carrey's Commencement Address with Transcript,"
   Motivation Mentalist, updated September 8, 2015, https://
   motivationmentalist.com/2015/09/08/jim-carrey
   -commencement-address-with-transcript/.

2. David Naylor, "Kill Your Status Quo Before It Kills You,"
   Forbes, June 11, 2018, https://www.forbes.com/sites/
   forbescoachescouncil/2018/06/11/kill-your-status-quo
   -before-it-kills-you/#3433da486a92.

3. Nathalie O'Neill, "Sheryl Sandberg's Newest Lean-In Effort:
   What Would You Do If You Weren't Afraid?" *Bustle,* June 5,
   2013, https://www.bustle.com/articles/26-sheryl-sandbergs
   -newest-lean-in-effort-what-would-you-do-if-you-werent-afraid.

4. Chris Barbin, "Do You Have a Vision? If You Have One, Is It
   Lame?" *Forbes*, February 5, 2018, https://www.forbes.com/sites/

forbestechcouncil/2018/02/05/do-you-have-a-vision-if-you
-have-one-is-it-lame/#3cec331c5620.

5. Corbett Barr, "Need Some Motivation Right Now? Read
This Immediately," *Fizzle*, January 23, 2018, https://fizzle.co/
sparkline/motivation.

6. Natalie Weiner, "Lauren Daigle on Her Grammy Nom and Why
She's a 'Rebellious' Christian Artist," *Billboard*, February 7, 2017,
https://www.billboard.com/articles/news/grammys/7684892/
lauren-daigle-grammy-nomination.

Hal Donaldson has authored thirty books and serves as founder and CEO of Convoy of Hope. He has degrees in journalism and biblical studies, and he and his wife, Doree, have four daughters.

Kirk Noonan serves as chief innovation officer for Convoy of Hope and has created innovative strategies to help people use their platforms to feed the hungry and help the suffering.

Lindsay Kay Donaldson is an attorney and member of Convoy of Hope's Communications team and a speaker for The Bravery Board, which promotes mental health and thriving to professionals and creatives.

FOR MORE INFORMATION ON CONVOY

OF HOPE, PLEASE VISIT

convoyofhope.org

WE'D LIKE TO STAY IN TOUCH. FIND
OUT MORE AND REACH US AT
haldonaldson.com